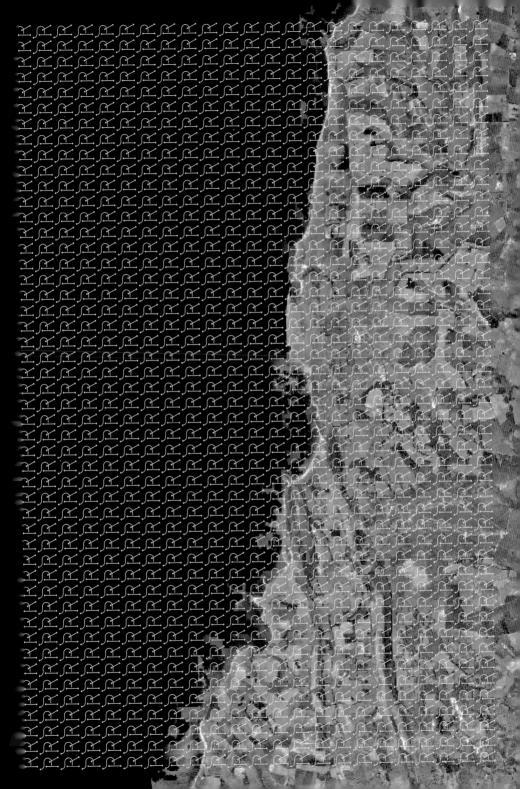

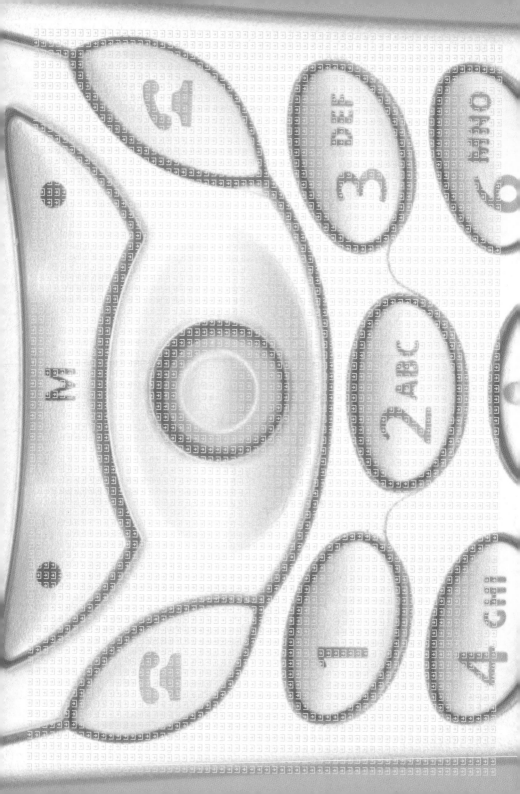

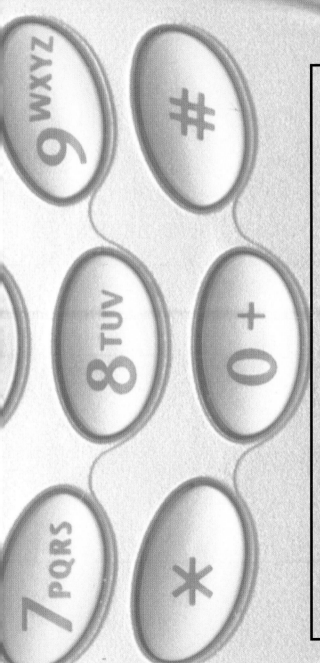

READER ON THE AESTHETICS OF MOBILITY   EDITED BY ANTHONY HOETE

BLACK DOG PUBLISHING LONDON NEW YORK

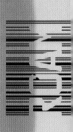

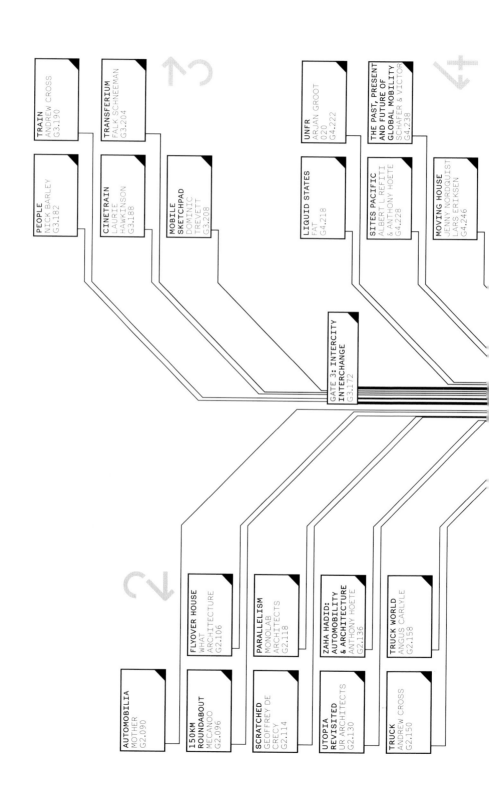

TRAIN
ANDREW CROSS
G3.190

TRANSFERIUM
FALK SCHNEEMAN
G3.204

PEOPLE
NICK BARLEY
G3.182

CINETRAIN
LAURIE
HAWKINSON
G3.188

**MOBILE
SKETCHPAD**
DOMINIC
TREVETT
G3.208

UNFR
ARJAN GROOT
020
G4.222

**THE PAST, PRESENT
AND FUTURE OF
GLOBAL MOBILITY**
SCHAFER & VICTOR
G4.238

LIQUID STATES
FAT
G4.218

SITES PACIFIC
ALBERT L REFITI
& ANTHONY HOETE
G4.228

MOVING HOUSE
JENNY NORDQUIST
LARS ERIKSEN
G4.246

**GATE 3: INTERCITY
INTERCHANGE**
G3.172

AUTOMOBILIA
MOTHER
G2.090

**150KM
ROUNDABOUT**
MECANOO
G2.096

FLYOVER HOUSE
WHAT
ARCHITECTURE
G2.106

SCRATCHED
GEOFFREY DE
CRECY
G2.114

PARALLELISM
MONOLAB
ARCHITECTS
G2.118

**UTOPIA
REVISITED**
UR ARCHITECTS
G2.130

**ZAHA HADID:
AUTOMOBILITY
& ARCHITECTURE**
ANTHONY HOETE
G2.136

TRUCK
ANDREW CROSS
G2.150

TRUCK WORLD
ANGUS CARLYLE
G2.158

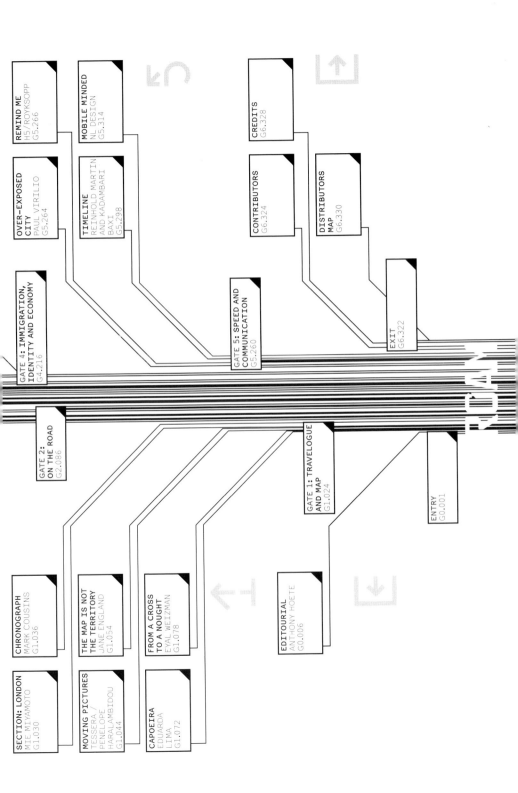

REMIND ME
H5/ROYKSOPP
G5.266

MOBILE MINDED
NL DESIGN
G5.314

CREDITS
G6.328

OVER-EXPOSED CITY
PAUL VIRILIO
G5.264

TIMELINE
REINHOLD MARTIN AND KADAMBARI BAXI
G5.298

CONTRIBUTORS
G6.324

DISTRIBUTORS MAP
G6.330

GATE 4: IMMIGRATION, IDENTITY AND ECONOMY
G4.216

GATE 5: SPEED AND COMMUNICATION
G5.260

EXIT
G6.322

GATE 2: ON THE ROAD
G2.086

GATE 1: TRAVELOGUE AND MAP
G1.024

ENTRY
G0.001

SECTION: LONDON
MIE MIYAMOTO
G1.030

CHRONOGRAPH
MARK COUSINS
G1.036

MOVING PICTURES
TESSERA / PENELOPE HARALAMBIDOU
G1.044

THE MAP IS NOT THE TERRITORY
JANE ENGLAND
G1.054

CAPOEIRA
EDUARDA LIMA
G1.072

FROM A CROSS TO A NOUGHT
EYAL WEITZMAN
G1.078

EDITOURIAL
ANTHONY HOETE
G0.006

editourial
anthony
hoete

Today we live, work and ROAM in a world of perpetual motion. The mobility of people, goods, information and services confronts, permeates and saturates our everyday existence.

To be able to relocate whatever, whenever, wherever to whoever suggests that mobility forms one image of contemporary society. Mobility is, however, more than a privileged vista. Having gathered momentum throughout the past century, the all-pervasiveness of mobility today is such that, in ROAM, the contemporary is only intelligible when seen from the condition of mobility.

In order to appreciate its pervasiveness, the context from which mechanical forms of mobility appeared needs to be briefly revisited. After the steam engine was invented in the early eighteenth century, various attempts were made to apply this source of power to self-propelled road vehicles. Techniques of industrialisation, and their consequential refinement through technology were, two hundred years later, exemplified by Henry Ford's introduction of the automobile production line. America, unlike Europe, had a distinct shortage of skilled labour and thus adopted a divergent approach to the innovative potential latent within the machine. British machine tools were massive, built to last and to serve any number of different purposes whereas American tools were small and designed with one particular task in mind. The interchangeability of parts, with precision components fitted by unskilled labour, became the quintessence of mass production. Detroit thus became Motown, the first major 'city on wheels', where every job was connected to the automotive industry. Mass production requires mass market consumption. Inside the factory, the employee was also the first customer/salesman and the immediacy of this interface resulted in accelerated sales. American manufacturers such as Ford, General Motors, Chevrolet, Dodge and Chrysler all flourished with the US accounting for 70% of the world's production of 13.2 million vehicles by

1 Motor Vehicle Manufacturer's Association (MVMA), *World Motor Vehicle Data*, 1989 Edition. www.geocities.com/MotorCity/Speedway/4939/carprod.html#country; Klein, Naomi, "New Branded World", *No Logo*, London: Flamingo, 2001, p 6.

1955 (though the emergence and dominating presence of Japan as a technological force had reduced the US market share to just 13% by 2000).[1]

Faced with a surplus of uniform mass produced goods, factories were forced to create unique identities for their product in order to compete for the consumer. Competitive branding became a necessity of the mechanised mobile age and with this the notion of the consumer society evolved.[2] Public announcements via brandspaces and billboards such as "the world's favourite airline", are today commonplace. In shaping the twentieth century, modernity was a phenomenon of simultaneous change and continuity. Its theories provide an endless loop of reformulation and reinterpretation, within which 'the contemporary' can be seen as a 'second modernism'; one linked with the emergence of information technologies and telecommunication. Today the mechanised space of modernism – of cars, trains and planes – has been overlaid by the electronic space, the bits and bytes, of 'modemism'.

Mobility, in the contemporary context, is a complex concept, ideologically elusive, difficult to pin down. Mobility is a transitory, transformational state, reconfigurable and self-refreshing, time after time. Mobility is an 'event-space', a sequence of appointments and rendezvous. Mobility is multi-dimensional in that it temporally functions beyond the x-y-z limits of Cartesian space. Mobility is polymorphous: its myriad forms include social mobility, automobility, mobile telephony and eco-tourism, to name but a few. Mobility incorporates information technologies and telecommunications triggering a spatial schizophrenia – today you can be in two places

2 Boomkens, Rene, "The 'Middle Landscape' and the Myth of Mobility: Coming Home in Commuter Country", The Urban Condition: Space, Community and Self in the Contemporary Metropolis, Rotterdam: 010 Publishers, 1999.

at once! Mobility is multi-scalar: as a concept it simultaneously envelops, for example, the global map of airspace, the specific scales of architectural space and the virtual world of communications. The history of mobility is thus the history of the use of cast iron and steel in architecture, the introduction of the elevator, the electrification of the railway system, the introduction of the automobile as a private means of transportation, the spread of air traffic, the invention of the refrigerated shipping container, and, finally, of the so-called revolution of informatics and telematics.[3] Mobility is also multi-linear. Whilst comprised of journeys from A to B, these lines constitute networks: from C to DE via KLM. As such mobility's multi-dimensionality suggests a matrix, or an array of co-ordinates.

3 Motorsat: www.emoto.com.

Multi-modality

A 'mode' is the vehicle for mobility. It is a transportational service, a means for the relocation of persons, goods and information: on foot, by car, train, plane or phone — and can either be public, private or, as is increasingly common today, a hybridised variant, such as a public-private partnership. Modes are thus a measure of the relative wealth of a society expressed in its infrastructural 'linescapes'. For the pedestrian these include pavements, footpaths, escalators and elevator shafts, whilst in the case of the automobile, linescapes materialise as mews, streets, highways, motorways and autobahn. Whilst not all modal lines are visible, all can be traced and mapped; airline flight paths, for example, are invisible trajectories. In a multi-modal transport system travellers have the liberty to chose from a combination of modes according to the spatial economics of journey planning and time trading. Whilst this is not novel, what makes multi-

modality symptomatic of contemporary mobility is the
variety and complexity of the vehicles available today
– as in the everyday example of talking on a cellular
whilst walking to the Underground.

4 IATA World Airline
Travel Statistics 46.

5 www.gsmworld.com.

6 www.baa.com/heathrow,
www.cityoflondon.
gov.uk.

The impact of self-powered modes of transportation upon
Western society can be measured in terms of ownership:
the 60 million vehicles of 1950 had accelerated to 535
million by 2000, or the equivalent of one vehicle each
for 9% of the world's population.[4] 32 years after the
Wright Brothers' first powered flight in 1903, the
first commercial passenger airliner took off, with
1,500 million people flying 240 billion kilometres by
the century's end.[5] Since then, the shift from the
modern into the contemporary is marked by technological
transformation – from mechanical to digital modes of
telecommunication. The first concept of a mobile phone,
initiated as a kind of two-way radio, was proposed
shortly after World War II. By the century's end there
were 722,000,000 cellular phone operators world-wide –
12% of the world's population were 'connected'.[6] The
global spread of this mode of mobility is, however, by
no means uniform. Within certain nations of the
European Union, the cellular proportion of the national
population reaches 85% whilst, surprisingly, in the
United States, the world's richest nation, this
proportion is a meagre 5%. For America, the automobile,
rather than the mobile, remains the modal choice of
the nation.

At The Interchange Of Mode: Node
A node is an intersection of two modes or two modal
lines and is, thus, a potential interchange. Some nodes
are materialised in space as railway stations,
airports, network hubs and, ultimately, cities. Others
are ephemeral in that they gather and dissipate leaving

no trace: queues and traffic jams are a veritable sign of the presence of mobility. Paradoxically, mobility infers immobility.

7 www.apim.com.

Nodes exist at various sizes and locations. Urban nodes typically consume large swathes of land, due to the open expanse of the infrastructural landscape of platforms, goods yards and railway lines (or gates, hangars and runways), with the enclosed spaces of a railway station or an airport terminal being relatively minor. In the case of a central railway station, the requisite platform configuration splays the modal lines of the rail with the resulting 'reverse bottlenecking' having dire urban consequences; large physical presence, little social interactivity. Airports are ordinarily on the outskirts of cities – edge nodes – because of sound restrictions and ground consumption. Heathrow Airport, the world's busiest airport in terms of passengers, covers 1,200 hectares, or an area four times the size of the City of London.[7] Beyond the urban and into the country, transferia nodes on major routes are fast appearing as the intercity rural interchange. A park-and-ride 'transcape'.

One of Newton's Laws of Motion states the greater the mass of a planet, the greater its gravitational pull. Similarly for a node, the greater its size, the greater its socio-economic pull. If the growth of a node accelerates, if its mobile programmes and infrastructures amass and economically accumulate at mega scales, a city agglomerates as a 'transmetropolis'. The Eurometropolis railway station that brought the high speed French train, the poignantly named Tres Grande Vitesse (TGV), to Lille, saw the transformation of an urban node by this high speed mode. The very fast urbanism of Lille attracts 20

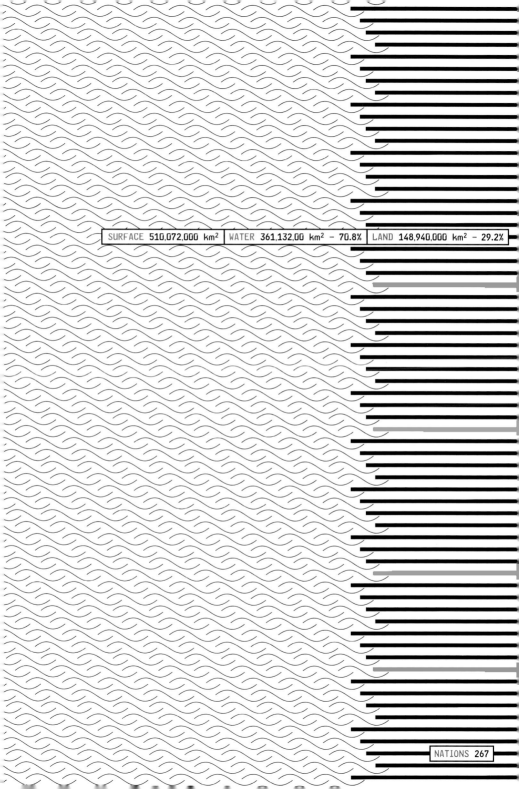

SURFACE 510,072,000 km² | WATER 361,132,00 km² — 70.8% | LAND 148,940,000 km² — 29.2%

NATIONS 267

million transit visitors through the city each year, with the 100 visitors for each inhabitant meaning that Lille is a city that functions as a transit lounge![8]

Someplace, Anywhere

If the city is perceived as a node, then the idea of travel incorporates, like the transit bearings characteristic to both maritime navigation and 'visual flight rules', an awareness of another place. If mobility can be viewed through immobility (the traffic jam, the airport queue), then, unsurprisingly, the concept of place can be defined via its diametric opposite. To be out of place is not to be in another place but somewhere in between. A 'non-place' is what Marc Augé terms the interstitial location between here and there, between two significant points and a meaningful existence. Non-places are detached from any localisation or social networks and tend to be anonymous — void of particularity — and inert to geographic position — airports, shopping malls, motorways, supermarkets, hospitals. Non-places carry no history, or "no history other than the last 48 hours of news".[9] Place has a historical context in which social relations evolve, with the opposition between place and non-place being reformulated as they arise. Place thus never disappears completely and, similarly, a non-place is never fully established; a palimpsest in which an elusive game of identity is being enacted. Non-places turn the subject into a passenger, a user, a customer, or listener, identified by name, address, date of birth, passport and PIN number.

One intention for architecture has been to ground space to place: to be site-specific. Yet within the contemporary maelstrom of easy jet travel and world-wide surfing, what value today resides in 'making a

8 Auge, Marc, *Non-Places: Introduction to an Anthropology of Supermodernity,* London: Verso, 1995.

9 Auge, Marc, "From Place to Non-Place", *Culture and Globalisation Reader,* 1995.

place' or forging a localised identity? Has the non-place with its anonymous, anywhere fabric of generic main streets and jargon branding meant that specificity and locality will increase as a common currency? Mobility is concerned with how one occupies the duration between places. In the void of travel, the passenger 'kills time'. Waiting, sleeping, reading, texting and calling are all non-events that typify the journey between home and office. Spatial mobility thus resolves not only the logistics and objectives of getting people, goods, services and information from A to B but accepts that the place you are at is the ideal place to be part of: a transitory experience.

Spatial Mobility

Space fractures and multiplies the question of mobility, ranging in type from the urban to the domestic, from the architectural to the geopolitical and socio-economic. The typical journey is a Venn Diagram of intersecting and overlapping spaces with the daily home-to-work journey showing the domestic ceding to the urban, overlaid by the economies of the ticket price. Meanwhile, cellular coverage fades in and out. Mobility territorialises space by allowing the 'passenger' to experience a number of spatial thresholds.

The urban space of modernism has influenced architectural production, resulting in a built environment with more light and a more adaptable organisation. Although this view of spatial mobility was framed by increasing the circulation through open planning, other perspectives were completely missed. Immobilities arose: the fixing of function to form; the static aesthetic of white walls. Mobility problematises architecture because, whilst buildings stand still,

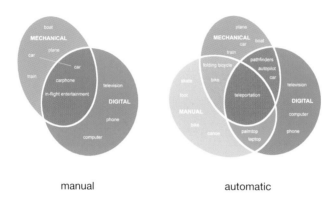

manual   automatic

In the 'Venn Diagram of Mobility', modalities are considered as either manually, mechanically or digitally powered forms of transportation. At the outset, all modes require at least an initial manual impulse or trigger. The car, for example, is a mechanised form whose engine is ignited through a hand turning a key. However, with technological advancements, manual impulses and actions are gradually ceding, along a sliding scale, to the desires of automation. In our increasingly mobilised world, today's driver is tommorow's passenger.

people and the contexts within which they are situated
do not. To engage with a mobilised idea of space
represents a fundamental shift away from that which was
once fixed to that which is today 'fluxed', ephemeral
or fluid. If architecture is to remain relevant in
respect to our ever increasing mobility, then the
foundations for building have to be reconsidered as
severed and uprooted.

If mobility appears in various guises and forms, then
the complete picture of a contemporary *mobilised*
architecture will always remain partially obscured
from view. Since modernism clarified certain
technological issues surrounding the 'buildability' of
architecture – for example, pre-stressed concrete
providing larger spans and structural glazing
dissolving enclosed space – the advent of digital
spaces in design mean that the question changes from
"Can we build it?" to "Can we see it?" Blurred
buildings and invisible architectures – cities
designed as motion perception drive-through or fly-by
sequences – result from the dissolution and
reintegration of conventional representations of
mobility. Architecture's embracing of digital
technologies has resulted in something paradoxically
more visual in its aesthetic yet less visible in terms
of its meaning.

The 'Venn Diagram of Mobility' intersects many other
spaces including the psychological and physiological.
Spatial schizophrenia reappears as the difference
between time zones, breaking down what is familiar. As
Jean Baudrillard has remarked, a passenger on Concorde
may actually arrive in New York before he left Paris.
The phenomenon of jet-lag, whereby the biological time
of the body is being upset by time differences between

the place of departure and the place of destination,
adds to the impression of the air journey as unreal and
somewhat magical: it transcends nature – it brackets
and relativises time and space. Not all motionary
effects are, however, desirable. After a 27 hour flight
the consequences of being in transit include fatigue,
blocked ears, motion sickness and the deep vein throb
of economy class syndrome. Frustration and nervousness
accompany the waiting and resulting delays: welcome to
the world of mobility without movement.

The measure of mobility today is the measure through
which we value our place in contemporary society.
Mobility is an indicator of quality of life and thus
links in with a broader concept of social theory. To
roam is to travel over or through a broad space. ROAM
reinforces this view of mobility through a cross-
disciplinary platform including art, architecture,
urbanism, film, and philosophy; with mobility as a
sectional sequence that transgresses the boundaries of
architecture, the city and the state.

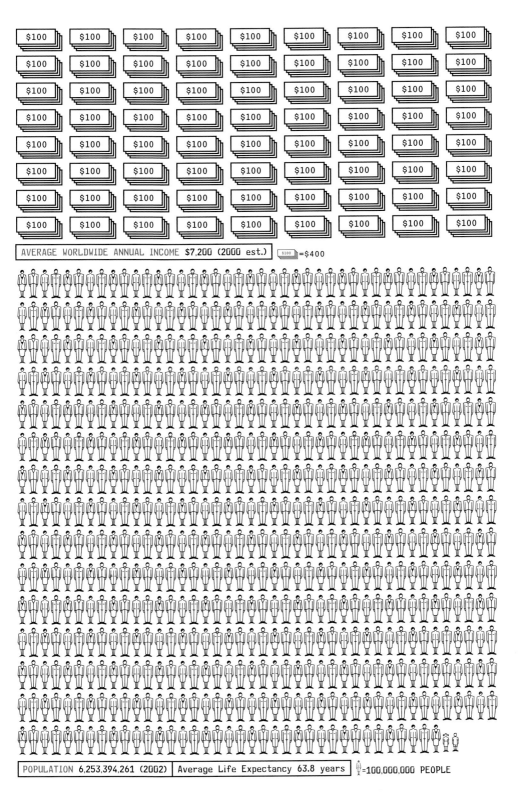

AVERAGE WORLDWIDE ANNUAL INCOME $100 = $400

AVERAGE WORLDWIDE ANNUAL INCOME $7,200 (2000 est.) $100 = $400

POPULATION 6,253,394,261 (2002) | Average Life Expectancy 63.8 years | = 100,000,000 PEOPLE

GATE
ONE

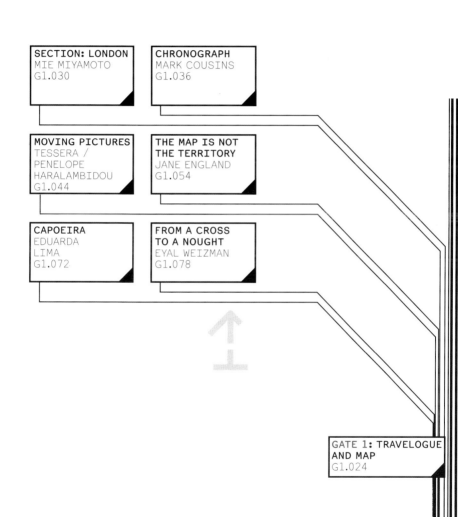

SECTION: LONDON
MIE MIYAMOTO
G1.030

CHRONOGRAPH
MARK COUSINS
G1.036

MOVING PICTURES
TESSERA /
PENELOPE
HARALAMBIDOU
G1.044

THE MAP IS NOT
THE TERRITORY
JANE ENGLAND
G1.054

CAPOEIRA
EDUARDA
LIMA
G1.072

FROM A CROSS
TO A NOUGHT
EYAL WEIZMAN
G1.078

GATE 1: TRAVELOGUE
AND MAP
G1.024

travelogue
and map

In his essay "The Storyteller" Walter Benjamin suggests that traditionally there have been two kinds of story: those that remain localised and pass on traditions (the shopkeeper, the market trader, the postman) and those that recount journeys to and from places afar (Genghis Khan, Marco Polo).[1] The narrative accounts that arise through movement and relocation empower the travelogue as a provocative means to bridge here with there. Once upon a time explorers sought new-found lands, combining maps and travelogues to form geographic diaries. Foreign cities and distant places thus became time-based reconstructions.

1 Benjamin, Walter, "The Storyteller", Illuminations, Hannah Arendt, ed, Harry Zohn, trans New York: Schoken Books, 1969.

Benjamin crucially depicts any travel record as open to interpretation: the travelogue rests on the selective recounting of distant events rather than their explanation. Loaded with the pretence of factual documentary, the log of a journey will always, in part, be a landscape of fabrication and evocation. The map is by no means an accurate account; they are coloured by the aspirations and perspective of the cartographer. The pan-urban recording of the city by a pedestrian observer in Mie Miyamoto's *Section: London* certainly doesn't resonate with the objective authority of a map. The city is sliced and exposed by a walk, constructing a grounded view rather than the remote, overhead, 'all-seeing' vantage point of a traditional map. The eye in the sky is so detached that the city, as blocked, say, in the Nolli plan of Rome, is shown devoid of citizenry. *Section: London* is a populated mapping of the social and public spaces of the city: people going about their business. This view suggests that the city might best be understood and designed in section — the plane of perception — rather than in plan — the plane of construction. The walk, here, constitutes a pop-up sequencing of the city in four dimensions.

In the Tessera project *Transient Field* the ground of a city square becomes a zone of manipulation and reinterpretation. Their design for a square in Zurich adapts to the impulses of passers-by who, during the day, can rearrange sliding panels to form seating, alcoves of intimacy and playground equipment. At night the square's ground transforms into a luminous pixilated screen. The project is an 'active' map: a giant horizontal screen that becomes a framed space for social encounters in which illuminated pedestrians traverse and engage with each other and/or the pre-programmed uses that lie embedded within its structure. Maps that refuse to try to fully capture

The Portuguese Pedestrian Manifesto denounces the modernisation of the pedestrian as represented in signs found on public streets. The high level of 'iconisation' is seen to result in a loss of identity. Yet within the constraints, rules and regulations demanded for global standardisation, some geo-cultural variance still emerges.

Portugal

Netherlands

Spain

Luxembourg

Italy

Italy

UK

Portugal

Italy

France

space compensate by pursuing and creating events, mobilising the viewer to a higher level of engagement with their surroundings.

Interpretative disciplines, such as art, have appropriated the map for ulterior motives. In "The Map is Not the Territory", Jane England shows how the artist/ explorer creates new maps that take us on journeys, questioning how we encounter and translate the world. Here landscapes are fabricated, with the ascendance of the map in art beginning in the modernist era, sharing modernism's concerns with organising, co-ordinating and ordering. Depictions of the city, however, have resisted this tendency to charter the visibly material through maps of psychogeographical terrain rather than physical topography. Maps depicting itineraries and travelogues become methods for recording new ways of experiencing the environment according to the structure of movement, time and mood.

Finally, in this section of ROAM, the changing of a traffic light in Eyal Weizman's "From a Cross to a Nought" refers allegorically to different phases within urban time: the multiplicity of rhythms yields a node of regulated transition that infiltrates and permeates the adjacent urban fabric by turning a signaled intersection into a giant roundabout.

The representation and re-enactment of movement is crucial to our understanding of mobility. The travelogue and map combine to impregnate space with event. Such a time-based reading configures the space of mobility as the space of duration. The aesthetic of mobility is thus episodic — not a moment of frozen space, but a continuous and mutative sequence of spaces.

France

France

Italy

Mexican Border, USA

Scotland

Italy

Spain

Portugal

France

France

France

Scotland

section:
london
mie
miyamoto

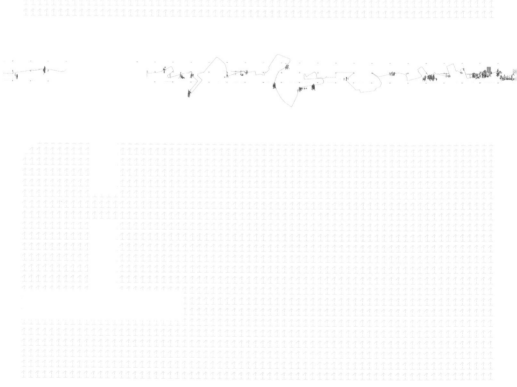

Section: London is the recording of a specific
journey within London. This journey, entirely on
foot, traces an artificial trajectory — a
straight line drawn on a map — from Whitechapel,
in East London to Ealing, in the West: a distance
of some 17.6 kilometres.

chronograph

mark

cousins

Photography erupted into experience partly as an
incitement to the human being to consider the passage of
time. This ancient philosophical motif does not throw
light upon the techniques of photography itself, but it
does highlight the major way in which photography was
seized upon in the silent, anonymous ritual of its
consumption, as an element within remembrance. The
haunted ordinariness of photography came to involve the
relation or the passage which it established between a
then and a now. The idea of a then was no longer the
property of an internal function of memory, the memory
of that which is predicated upon a specific then. The
idea of a then was now exteriorised and printed upon the
paper which I gaze at now. And indeed, as I gaze I also
think that it can outlast me, this then, without me in a
now, when I am no longer. These thens built up in the
countless personal archives, ostensibly of the subject:
the family, the marriage, the forgotten colleague, the
unrecalled picnic, the subsequently sold home, complete
strangers crossing the background of the photograph,
that seat, those clouds... gradually the photograph
caught the imagination of the population and installed
itself as a popular reflection on the passage of time.
The indexability of photography bequeathed internal
life with a new medium of loss.

In order to play this role photography exhibits a
fundamental stillness – a stillness which evacuates time
from the internal character of the photograph. Of course
photography requires that the photographic paper is
exposed to light over a precise length of time, but this
passage of time belongs to the order of technique rather
than the order of the experience of photography. That
experience is dominated by the moment, by the minimum
unit of time required to support the category of an
event. It is registered by the 'click' of the camera, a
vanishing point of duration, an event which occurs in

time but is not represented by time. It is as if this
stillness of the image is a kind of cross-section of
time, a moment. The stillness is related to the draining
away of time from the image in order to supply the full
representation of space. The photographed moment
captures space in a piercing fashion, in a way in which
the harassed character of perception can rarely do. The
stillness of the image is the effect of a particular
distribution of time and space. As a cross-section of
time the image does not embody time but rather space,
which is opened up. The image tends towards the character
of a still life, which is still, not because of the
motionless character of the scene, but because time has
been exteriorised, away from the image and towards the
spectator. Indeed perhaps it is not ridiculous to extend
the idea of the stillness of the image to the movies
themselves. Of course movies represent movement but do
so exclusively through the space of the image, through
the sequence of the cross sections of time which have
emptied the image of duration. The movie takes time, may
even represent time, but does so through a sequence of
images which are based upon the fundamental stillness of
space, in which even movement appears as a series of
images which are stilled by their exhaustion in space.
The question is not how are space and time represented
in images, but how do spatially organised images – for it
is those, which we are used to – represent time?

Rather than try to answer this, the whole question can
be turned around. If the stillness of the images is the
result of the spatialisation of time, could one imagine
something different, perhaps even the opposite? It
would be a type of image in which time was taken back
into the interior of the image, no longer projected into
the observing subject, but dictating the form of the
image. And if this was the structure of this time/image,
what type of space would be represented? What would it

mean to displace the cross-section of time with a period of space? Perhaps the answers lie in these photographs by Christian Nicolas and Eyal Weizman. In a sense what they photograph is time, but that says no more than saying that other people photograph space. What is at issue is the redistribution of both time and space in respect to the photograph.

Nicolas and Weizman adapted a camera so that it had an open slot of one millimetre as its aperture. Behind this the film is run in a single exposure over a set time, that is at a set speed, usually about 15 to 40 seconds. The camera is still, only the film moves. How should one describe the result? In one sense a millimetre of space is spread out the length of the film — where length refers to time. Space is expelled from the image which can be thought of as the opposite of a panorama. What is

photographed is the space which is opened by the millimetre aperture — that is all that is photographed, but it is not still. The bodies which appear along the length of the image are not like those that we are used to reading, spread across the image because they occupy different places in space. For in fact all bodies in the image are in the same place, but they are in the same place at different times. What appears as spacing, indeed what is spacing in the image is the flow of time. Time is not now a cross-section, but is the movement of the film itself, the time which is embodied in the image. It is as if time provides a cross-section of space, that is the same space analysed by a passage of time.

If this procedure, which was developed from the
technique used in sports to register the winner of
races, seems to upturn the relations between time and
space in the photographic image, then we should not be
surprised at how difficult it is to incorporate its
results. Looking at the photographs will evoke a sense
of puzzlement and regression, which attempts to
reintegrate them in the previous model of the 'spatial
image'. Of course it can't be done, they won't fit. But
even the most elementary effects of this technique
unsettle our habitual literacy in respect to the
photograph. Imagine that something within the visual
field of the aperture would register as a stationary
dot; here it registers itself as a continuous line that
runs for the length (of time) of the image. By extension
(of time) a vertical line turns into a surface,
manifesting a temporal rather than spatial solidity.

It follows from this that the scale of an object is
related not to its volume but to its speed. A thin
body and a stretched body in the image refer to a
quick body and a slow body. All these effects pose
problems to an eye trained to read the image in spatial
terms, leading to incomprehension. It is possible to
speak of an unconscious resistance; even when one
understands the image intellectually one can be
overtaken by a sudden affective refusal to understand,
an emotional insistence on reading in the old way. This
should alert us to the fact that this technique harbours
a certain horror in its capacity to render time internal
to the image.

This capacity is pushed to the extreme in one of the effects of this photographic technique. When positioned on London Bridge with pedestrians walking in opposite directions or by a dual carriageway with cars speeding both ways, the camera produces the following result: all the bodies (or cars) are represented as travelling in the same direction. The bodies and cars that are travelling in the 'opposite' direction are folded into the image and appear to have their direction reversed. This effect is a tribute to the tenacity of our way of reading the image as the spatial image, in which directionality is a constitutive element. We have the feeling that some fundamental level of reality has been travestied, that the truth is in fact quite simple, or rather it can be simply put, even though it remains hard to grasp. When we speak of this technique of 'direction', the direction in question must be the direction in which the film is moving through the camera. It is the moving film that creates the singular direction which can only be measured in units of time. If a body is moving in the same direction as the film is travelling, say from left to right, there is no counter-intuitive effect. But if a body is travelling in the opposite direction to the film, its own direction will be erased in the following way: imagine that the first element of the body exposed to the film is the nose; by the time the next element, the eye, is exposed, the film will have travelled and if the eye is represented after the nose, the before and after refer only to one direction, that is the direction in which the film is travelling. Another way of putting this is that we are used to thinking of direction as necessarily involving two directions, say left and right. It seems a primordial fact about the world and about images that there is a left and right just as there was for Aristotle, together with a below and an above, a before and behind. The orientation of the body,

and likewise the legibility of the image both seem to
demand these dimensions. But this image of London Bridge
has only one direction, that of time, and it is time
which determines the space of the image. This technique
renders time internal to the image where it re-orders
the space. This is where the horror is. Is everyone
walking in the same direction if I stand on London
Bridge? That depends. Spatially they are not; but if the
only dimension of measurement is that of time, then they
are. But where are they going, all in the same direction?

In the traditional photographic image the question of
time is attached to the image but is absent from it as
a moment of space. The temporal relations in which the
image is caught up belong to the order of the
spectator, to the melancholy passage of time between
the point of original exposure and the point of its
viewing. It speaks of death in the form of mortality, of
human finiteness which is measured against the image,
whose youth increases each year. Death here is related
to the passing of time. But in this other technique,
where time determines the image, death erupts in the
order of the spacing of the image itself. They are all
going in the same direction, herded together, trekking
to what can only be death. We already know in
premonition that to see such a cowed march of massed
humans travelling together in the same direction has a
single, if secret, destination. Dragooned by the
military authority of time, they exhibit the passive
demeanour of fatality. If, in the image, time does
indeed become an arrow, we fall back appalled by its
speed, by the inflexible accuracy of its trajectory,
and by the lethal singularity of its target – death. No
one escapes, and as befits a technique borrowed from
the photofinish of races, everyone is a winner as the
subject who is first past the post when it comes to
death. No contest.

moving
pictures
tessera

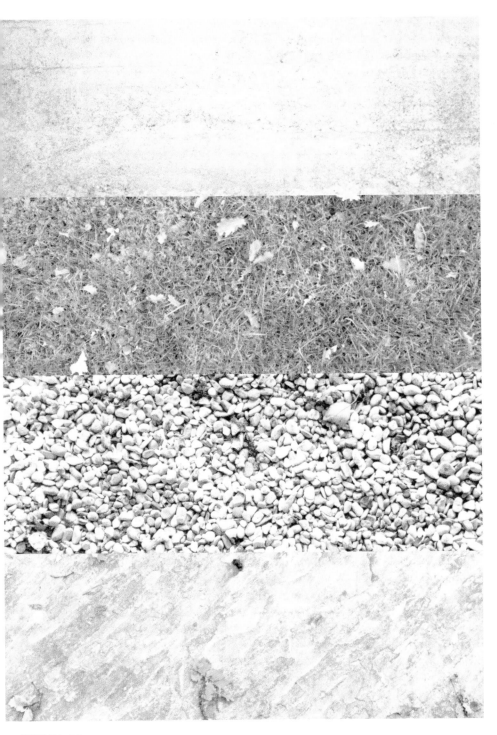

The Intrusion of Chance

Tessera attempts to question the conventional conception of space in an ideal state of rest; the stagnant architecture which surrounds us. Through two proposals the notion of space as a dynamic field is explored through an architecture which presupposes narrative, transition and movement as the essence of spatiality. The loose and indeterminate nature of such an architectural approach reflects the complex and nomadic nature of our spatial experience.

The everyday experience of the built environment often leads us into a perceptual inertia and a feeling of boredom. The intrusion of shock and accident as a design method shakes our perceptual and aesthetic habits, awakens our spatial awareness and stimulates our imagination. In these proposals chance is accepted as a creative tool, producing new situations, operating as a complementary design device. Here the incident of chance can reveal a confusing, messy, tasteless and even dysfunctional side of spatiality. In this way architectural conventions – such as order, harmony, elegance and functionality – can be upset, extending and reinventing the means of a design language.

This 'unsettled' architecture periodically blossoms; surprising, stimulating and enriching our experience in a way that is similar to the effects of nature. The proposed schemes attempt to expose the play between the natural and the built environment, bridging the two, usually conflicting, conditions of living either in the country or in the city. Syntagma Square forms an experience of the 'urban forest', while Sechelauten-Platz constitutes Zurich's 'urban field'.

Ground view:
two elements, poles and hats,
form a perforated enclosure.

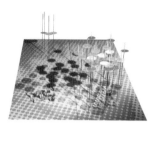  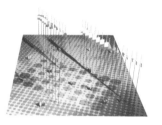

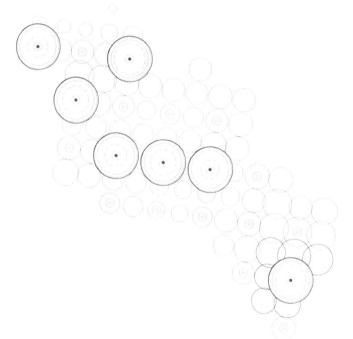

↑↑ The Urban Forest is
reconfigurable according
to seasons or events within
the city.

↑ Plan diagram of the Urban
Forest. This 'pilotis
architecture' of minimal
ground contact, occupancy
and usage where points
accumulated across the
ground, expand overhead to
form space. The pilotis was
upheld in the twentieth
century modernist
architecture of Le

Corbusier, today known as
"buildings on legs". As a
relocatable landscape ROAM
suggests that temporary
constructions (tensile
spaces such as tents and
umbrellas) can form large
yet mobile public spaces. In
the Urban Forest such space
forms a light perforated
image of an enclosure.

Urban Forest

Based on the spatial experience of the natural forest,
we proposed a flexible space that continuously
transforms the public function and image of Syntagma
Square. Through its performance, the Square "self-
composes" various spatial configurations and, thus,
always contains an element of surprise. The design
consists of vertical linear elements – the poles –
which support a number of floating light covers – the
hats. The pole and hat configuration changes depending
on the season, events and celebrations of the city. The
hats cast shadow patterns during the day and glow with
artificial light, illuminating the Square, at night.
The poles are arranged, as desired, on a grid of
sockets which relate to a half-tone typographic image,
enlarged to the size of the whole surface of the
Square. The image isolates an anonymous film still
from 1950s Greek cinema. It shows a typical Greek
"saloni", a symbolic icon of the 'public' life of the
Athenian house.

Relative transparency
of the Urban Forest.

↑One of the 'pixels' that
make up the floor of the
Transient Field.

↑Looping the pedestrian with
the car: the subterranean
parking structure is an
interface to pedestrian
square and a sliding
roof/floor.

Transient Field

During World War II the exposed earth of the Bellevue-Stadelhofen Square allowed the cultivation of potato and rape, an image deeply engraved in the collective memory of the city of Zurich. Today it facilitates traditional events such as the burning of the snowman, the installation of the circus and the alternation of seasonal markets. Our project keeps and reinterprets this rural character of the Square. We proposed the construction of a sliding floor which enables the transformation of the square into an even surface, a carrier of contemporary urban uses. This new floor is composed of panels arranged in long parallel strips which slide, creating various configurations between two extreme conditions: the absolutely empty — revealing the field — and the fully covered. The folding panels produce adaptable equipment: benches, low walls, playgrounds, etc.. At night the floor becomes a luminous horizontal screen, with the coloured panels as the pixels. They render either images of past memories or advertise future events on the whole stretch of the surface.

Overhead views of sliding
roof/floor which operates
under two conditions: open
or closed.

The upper side of the sliding roof forms
a public floor that is further fragmented
through sliding panels.

the map is not the territory

jane england

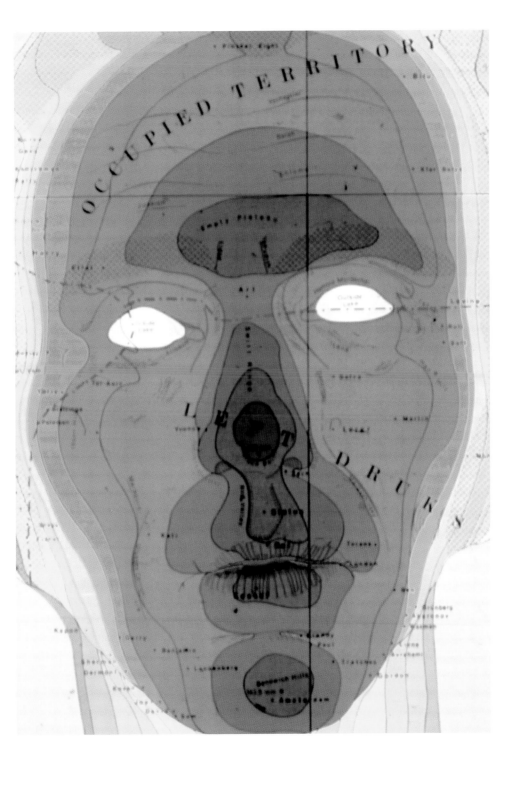

To roam is to be mobile — able to move freely from one place or position in the environment to another. The essential companion to mobility is orientation, the knowledge of distance and direction in relation to your surroundings, together with the ability to keep track of spatial relationships as they change while you move about. Maps provide the orientation that accompanies mobility so that you can reach where you want to go, or know exactly where it is that you have ended up: "You have taught me the fear of becoming lost.... In strange cities I memorise streets and always know exactly where I am. Amid scenes of great splendour, I review the route back to the hotel."[1]

1 Keillor, Garrison "95 Theses 95", *Lake Wobegon Days*, London: Faber & Faber, 1985, p 254.

←←Michael Druks
Druksland Physical and Social 15 January 1974, 11.30am, 1974
Lithograph, 46 x 38cm. Edition of 250.

Maps are read as a universal language, as representations of reality, with everyday accepted codes of symbols that are understood worldwide. They are a way of comprehending and dealing with notions of space, and a method of charting ideas and gathering and ordering knowledge. We form 'mental maps' of places by our selective processing of information in relation to our personal preferences and perceptions of the environment – a 'geography of perception' that is important in many daily decisions, such as where to live, where to travel, where to avoid, where to shop, and where to site new buildings and towns.[2] Actual maps provide visual expression of our need to define our physical world and its boundaries.

These boundaries shift and change: individual cultures and geographic identities are modified by the increasingly mobile forces of economic, political and social globalisation. In response to this globalisation of culture, and as a way of dealing with their own place in the world, artists have become increasingly interested in using the visual language of maps alongside map-making strategies and systems – they recognise how "individuals, in a world where traditional geographic hierarchies and borders are in rapid transformation… are forced to navigate according to their own experiences".[3]

Jean Baudrillard wrote that "it is… the map that precedes the territory", but the title of this essay, *The Map is Not the Territory*, is taken from a phrase that was 'appropriated' from the philosopher and mathematician Alford Korzbski by the British artist Ralph Rumney, who later used the phrase as the generic title for many of his works and as a conceptual overview.[4] Rumney's *The Leaning Tower of Venice*, first published in 1958, was an illustrated essay on

2 Gould, Peter and White, Rodney, *Mental Maps*, Harmondsworth: Pelican Books, 1974, p 16.
3 Hoholt, Stine, "Introduction", *Clockwise – New Nordic Art*, Denmark: Arken Museum of Modern Art, 2002.
4 Baudrillard, Jean, *Simulacra and Simulation*, Sheila Faria Glaser, trans, Ann Arbor: The University of Michigan Press, 1994.

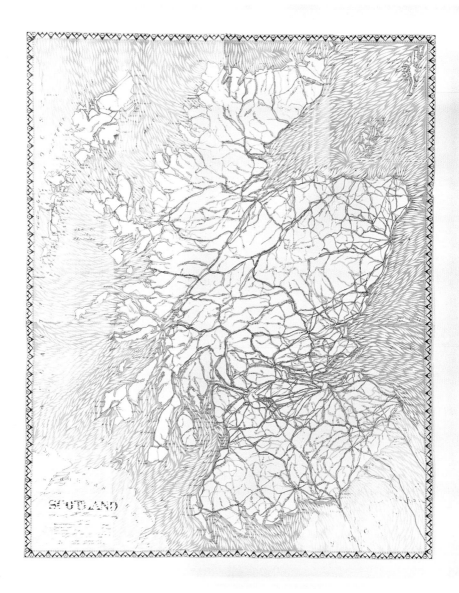

Georgia Russell
Scotland Skeleton, 2001.
Cut map in perspex box, 52 x 43 x 10cm.

psychogeography, the theory and practice of drifting or roaming through an urban environment. Like Guy Debord with his 1956 *Guide Psychogéographique de Paris*, Rumney took a Situationist approach to 'mapping' a city. He described it as "just wandering about and keeping your eyes open a bit, looking. You can walk down streets hundreds of times, then suddenly notice something you've never seen before, which suddenly changes your whole attitude to the street."[5] Rumney and Debord had no 'route-planner', no literal map – they explored cities informally, documenting their *dérives* with photographs and text observations.

The extensive use and popularity of the map in twentieth century art really began in the 1960s and 70s. Minimalist artists, concerned with numbers, time, measurement, and with tabulating data, used maps, topographical charts and cartographic procedures as a way of establishing order. Land and Conceptual artists "adopted the map and the photograph as evocative substitutes for first-hand experience", finding that their "compactness offered a more effective embrace of vast space than did constructed earthworks" – maps were a way to represent their activities.[6] Writing in the 1980s, art historian Lucy R Lippard pointed out how the map offers "a language through which to appreciate, without depicting, landscape. It is a way of modernising the whole notion of art about space."[7]

Maps and globes have been used by artists as symbolic emblems for centuries – to represent power in portraits of kings and statesmen, and as a way of indicating sovereignty over territory. In 1533 Hans Holbein used both celestial and terrestrial globes as symbols in his painting *The Ambassadors*. Jan Vermeer painted a map of the Netherlands within his work *The Artist's Studio* of 1665-1667 to suggest the area where the reputation of

5 Rumney, Ralph, interview, *Vague*, 1989/90.
6 Lippard, Lucy R, *Overlay: Contemporary Art and the Art of Prehistory*, New York: Pantheon Books, 1983.
7 Lippard, *Overlay*.

the artist could spread. In the time before the world was thoroughly mapped, cartography was an example of 'knowledge as power'. This knowledge rested with an elite few, and was seen as a 'science of princes'.

Maps of countries and states impose and provide borders that often have no basis in the actual geography of the land. They can delineate, define and influence the existence of the very concepts of a nation, an empire, or political divisions — Stephen Hall described maps as "worldviews committed to paper".[8] The map historian J B Harley saw maps as manifestos for a set of beliefs about the world. He said that "map making was one of the specialised intellectual weapons by which power could be gained, administered, given legitimacy, and codified"; and that maps have been used to express "the reality of conquest and empire".[9] The state and the military have always been principal patrons of cartography, and at its height the British Empire was defined by red areas on the world map. Maps change to accommodate political shifts — the red areas on world maps have shrunk along with the British Empire.

In an absurdist vein, Borges's story *Of Exactitude in Science* is about an empire in which "the craft of cartography attained such Perfection that the map of a Single Province covered the space of an entire city, and the Map of the Empire itself an entire province. In the course of Time, these Extensive maps were found somehow wanting, and so the College of Cartographers evolved a Map of the Empire that was on the same Scale as the Empire and that coincided with it point for point."[10]

In 1893 Lewis Carroll had written along the same lines, about "the *largest* map that would be very useful":

8 Hall, Stephen S, *Mapping the Next Millennium: The Discovery of New Geographies*, New York: Random House, 1992.

9 Harley, J B, "Maps, Knowledge and Power", in "The Iconography of Landscape: Essays on the symbolic representation, design and the use of past environments", *Cambridge studies in historical geography*, vol 9, Denis Cosgrove and Stephen Daniels, eds..

10 Borges, J L, *Of Exactitude in Science*, 1933-34, cited by Paul Melia, *Peter Greenaway, Artworks 63-98*, Manchester: Manchester University Press, 1988.

... And then came the grandest idea of all! We actually made a map of the country, on the scale of *a mile to a mile*! "Have you used it much?" I enquired. "It has never been spread out, yet," said Mein Herr; "the farmers objected: they said that it would cover the whole country, and shut out the sunlight! So we now use the country itself, as its own map, and I assure you it does nearly as well."[11]

Jonathan Swift's map of the island of Balnibarbi in *Gulliver's Travels*; Robert Louis Stevenson's map of *Treasure Island*; Arthur Ransome's map in *Swallows and Amazons*, E H Shepherd's *The World of Pooh*, and Tolkien's map in *The Lord of the Rings*, are examples of maps used to clarify fictional worlds. *The Redstone Diary of True Places*, published in 1997, took its title from Herman Melville's *Moby Dick*: "It is not down in any map; true places never are…". In his introduction to the *Redstone Diary*, Mel Gooding wrote that "all maps… are projections and imaginings, fictional grids and configurations cast like invisible nets over the intractable trueness of real worlds…".[12]

For centuries maps have mainly been seen as scientific exercises, but almost every map has an inherent visual appeal in its own right: the craft of cartography has applied aesthetics to science. Maps are so ubiquitous, so necessary to navigate the world, so visually appealing, and so comprehensive in their potential that it was inevitable that artists would be inspired to produce their own maps, and to utilise maps and concepts of cartography. Consequently it is possible to trace and roam along a trail through twentieth century art history to the present day; a trail through real and imagined geography.

11 Carroll, Lewis, *Sylvie and Bruno*, 1889.

12 Gooding, Mel, "True Places", *The Redstone Diary of True Places*, London: Redstone Press, 1996.

→→Kathy Prendergast
Lost, 1999.
Computer generated image on paper,
80 x 132.5cm. Edition 9 of 25.

ROAM/**G1.62**

K. Prendergast 1996

To start a tour of some random points along this trail, we can begin in the Swiss city of Berne, where around 1910 the schizophrenic 'outsider' artist Adolf Wölfli was drawing extraordinary 'inner' maps and maps of cities in his psychiatric hospital cell. Wölfli was not part of any art movement, but his maps formed an important part of his very individual mythology.

13 "Surrealist Map of the World", *Variétés*, 1929.

14 Graham Gussin, quoted in information sheet about *Ghost*, London, The Multiple Store, 2002.

In 1929 the Surrealists produced their own *Map of the World,* letting their imagination decide what was important — the Pacific Ocean is central, Australia is dwarfed by New Guinea, there is no United States of America, a tiny Africa is attached to a vast Russia, and so on.[13] In a similar vein, British artist Simon Faithfull has recently made a map that turns the world on its head: what was water has become land; what was land has become water. As he points out, "what should be a tool to interpret the world has become untrustworthy; what was familiar is now skewed and strange".

From the 1930s through to the 1950s, Joseph Cornell made box constructions that contain magical universes in microcosm, often using star charts and maps to evoke an ancient past when star-gazers searched for constellations. A later poetic and evocative use of star maps is Graham Gussin's *Ghost* of 2002, a work that started as a copy of *The Cambridge Atlas of the Stars,* was pulped and re-cast as a wall-mounted disc, with the original book and its contents rendered invisible. Gussin was "fascinated by the process of turning a map of the infinite reaches of space into a single block of material".[14]

Piet Mondrian was inspired by the grid of New York streets in his painting *Broadway Boogie-Woogie* of 1942-1943. Mondrian has in turn inspired Chris Kenny's recent series of collage constructions. In Kenny's *Street*

Drawings, map sections of various cities inscribed
with the names of streets are mounted on pins and placed
in arrangements that echo Mondrian's paintings of the
last century.

In 1943 Uruguayan artist Joaquin Torres-Garcia drew an
Upside-down Map of South America with the South Pole at
the top of the world, in order to suggest that South
America was an avant-garde rival to Paris and New York;
while in 1975 Saul Steinberg famously depicted the *New
Yorker View of the World*, with New York as the centre of
the universe.

In the 1960s, Pop artists such as Jasper Johns and Claes
Oldenberg became interested in using maps: Johns
deconstructed images of flags and maps in his paintings,
and Oldenberg made a soft sculpture map of Manhattan.
Fluxus artists George Brecht, Meiko Shiomi and Yoko Ono
used maps in their projects in the 1960s, and often used
mail art as a working method: Robert Watts' *Fluxatlas* of
the 1970s was a box containing collated and labelled
stones sent from many international locations. Yoko
Ono's *Map Piece* of 1962 consisted of instructions such
as "Draw an imaginary map" and "The map must be followed
exactly, or the event has to be dropped altogether."

Artists of the Italian Arte Povera movement such as
Lucio Fabro and Alighiero Boetti incorporated maps into
their works of the 1970s and 80s. Fabro made a series of
sculptures portraying the easily recognisable shape of
Italy in various materials; while Boetti produced
tapestry maps in Afghanistan with the collaboration of
local weavers in which political maps of the world were
filled in with flag symbols denoting nations.

Since the late 1960s British artists Richard Long and
Hamish Fulton have used text, maps and photographs to

document their walks through the landscape, as when in
1968 Long presented a ten mile walk on Exmoor as a line
drawn on an ordnance survey map. Dutch artist Stanley
Brouwn stood on a street corner in 1962 and asked people
to explain how he could get to another part of town by
drawing directions for him on pieces of paper stamped
"this way Brouwn", which became the name of the
resulting collated work.

Israeli born artist Michael Druks produced a series of
works in the 1970s under the title *Flexible Geography* in
which he used geography as a coded international visual
language. In Belgium, Marcel Broodthaers altered titles
of existing maps to open them to new interpretations,
and in 1975 made an atlas, *La Conquete de L'Espace, Atlas
à l'usage des artistes et des militaires* in which each
chosen country was reproduced on a separate sheet as if
it was an island. Susan Hiller, an American artist based
in Britain, has used maps in various conceptual projects
since the late 1960s, in particular in her *Dream Mapping*
of 1974. Argentine artist Guillermo Kuitca has been
depicting city maps and domestic floor plans since 1987,
including an installation in New York in 1993 of 60
mattresses painted with road maps, made perhaps for
journeys in dreams.

In *The Great Bear* of 1992, Simon Patterson renamed the
stations on the classic 1930s map of the London
Underground, replacing them with the names of historic
figures, philosophers and saints, together with
contemporary celebrities such as footballers and
actors. His subversive version of the Underground map is
a parallel mode of travelling through famous names of
history and popular culture.

British artists Langlands & Bell have made a series of
works where they map the world using only the elegant

The Great Bear

Simon Patterson
The Great Bear, 1992.

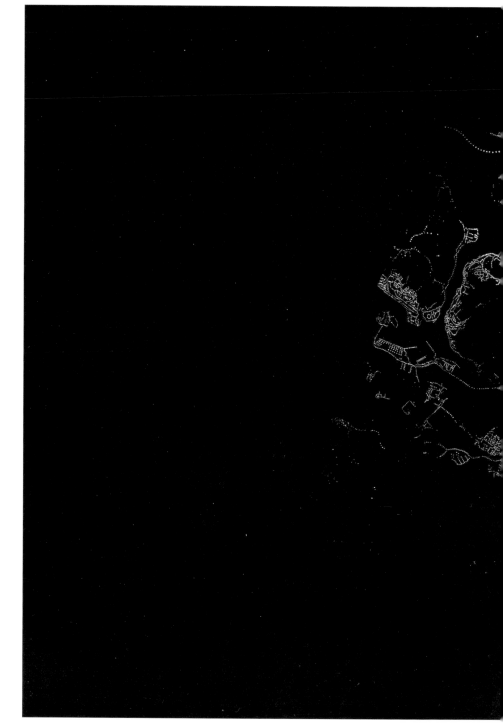

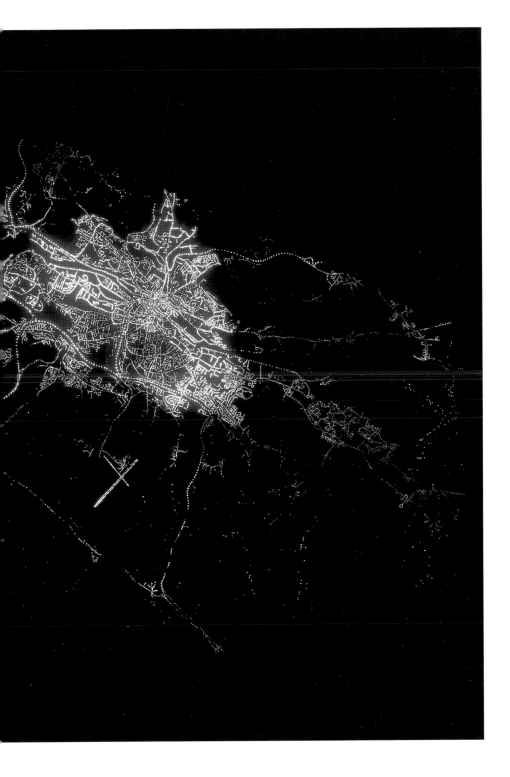

tracery of the air routes that link cities around the
globe. Jonathan Parsons literally dissected a map in his
Carcass of 1995, stripping away all but the arterial
roads of Britain. Along a similar line, Georgia Russell
uses a scalpel to cut away books and maps to produce
works such as her *Skeleton Map of Scotland*. Jason
Wallis-Johnson's light-box illuminations are maps made
by meticulously pin-pricking black carbon paper; the
resulting pierced surfaces shimmer like cities seen
from the air at night.

In 1998 Emma Kay drew two maps – *The World From Memory
I & II* – where, as in her other work, the subject was
really her own memory; the missing elements as important
as those recalled. Layla Curtis subverts maps of the
world: in works such as her *World Political* and *World
State* of 2001, she swapped and manipulated countries of
similar size and shape, producing new hybrid maps.
Belgian artist Wim Delvoye has made colourful maps of
non-existent places, and produced an *Atlas* of 'fake',
but logical-looking geography.

The possibilities of map making have been stretched
by new digital technology which has replaced the
hand-drawn maps and atlases of the past – artists
are now able to more easily manipulate cartography to
create their own new maps. Kathy Prendergast has
combined digital technology and place name information
on the internet to make works like *Lost*, a map of
America which only shows place-names with the prefix
"Lost", having deleted all others. Her current project,
An Emotional Atlas of the World, will show only names
connected with emotions, such as "Lonely Island" or
"Heart's Desire". Japanese artist Satomi Matoba's
seamless digital manipulations produce a map that
merges Pearl Harbour with Hiroshima; and in *Shores of a
River* she makes a convincing map of a totally re-made

←←Jason Wallis-Johnson
Portadown, 2001 (Detail).
Perspex light-box with pierced carbon paper,
35 x 28 x 8cm.

world with disturbing juxtapositions, saying that she "dissolves familiar maps in order to reconstruct the world, suggesting an open-ended potential within the act of shifting boundaries".

There are many more artists' geographies to explore than those touched on here, and over the past 30 years there have been several exhibitions around the world based on artists' maps. The historian Eric Hobsbawm said that "we need new maps if we are going to make sense of the world", and the artist-explorer, creating new maps, can take us on a journey that informs and enriches the way that we encounter and translate the world.

capoeira
eduarda
lima

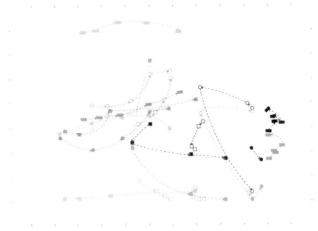

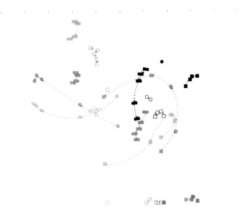

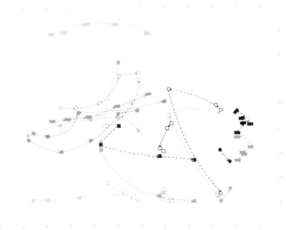

←←The interstitial space evolves and
mutates according to the interactivity
between the two players. A notational
diagram common to choreography offers an
alternate system in which to map player
location and thus movement.

→→Capoeira blends elements of dance,
music, acrobatics and martial arts into a
physical non-contact 'game' where one
approaches, yet ultimately, avoids touching
their opponent. Due to the rapidity of its
enactment, the relative speeds of various
bodily movements are not always registered.
The recording of such a body in motion is
captured here with the use of an open
shutter and moving film stock.

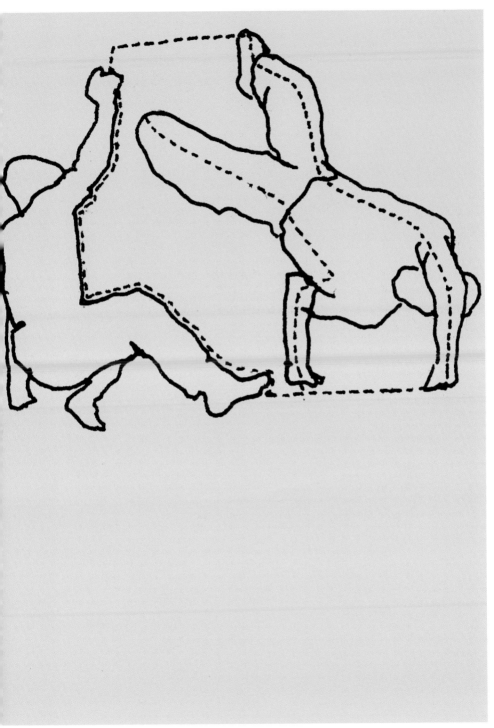

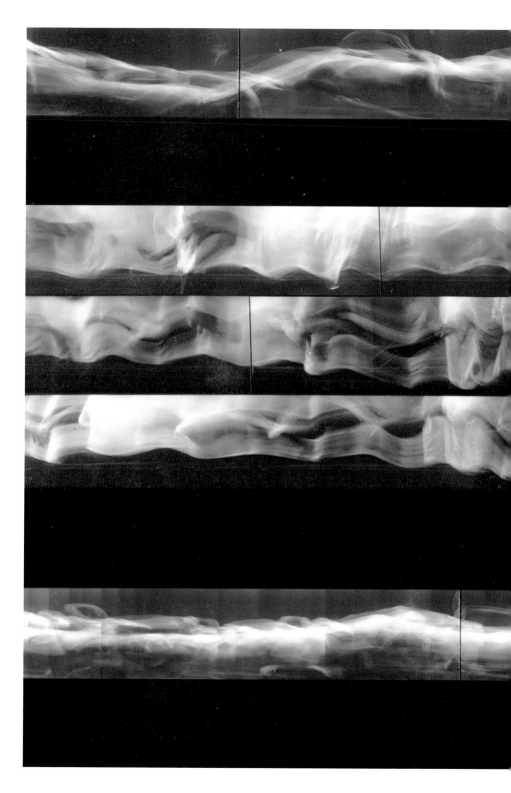

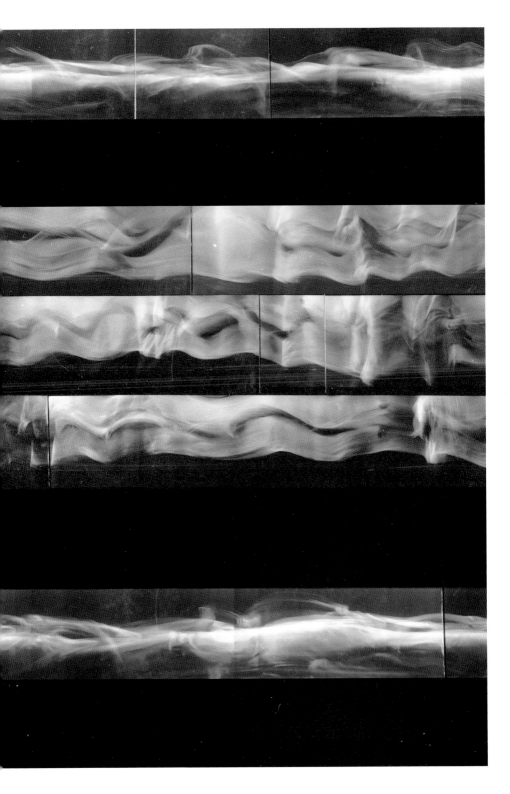

from a cross to a nought

eyal weizman

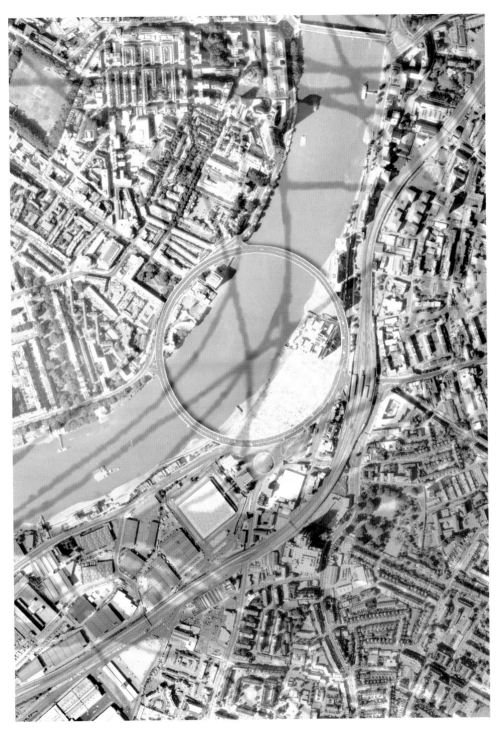

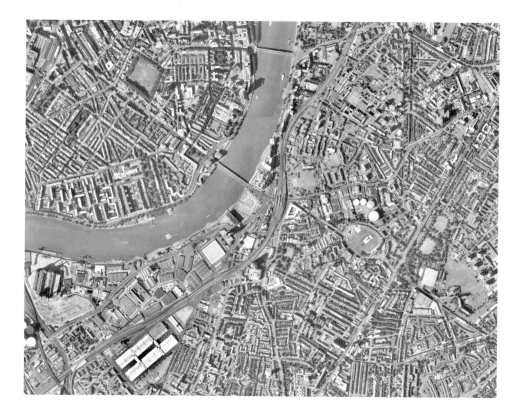

Vauxhall Bridge's deep abutments invade 50 metres into
the north bank of the Thames and 90 metres into the
south bank, forcing trunk roads A312 and A3036 back from
the river. The diverted roads allow for pockets of land
directly on the riverfront, making them extremely
desirable and expensive pieces of real estate. The
Government describes Effra, 2.94 hectares of empty land
located between Vauxhall Cross and the river, as the
"biggest and best-located real estate in the capital".
Though derelict until recently, for 50 years this site
has been drawing in the complex strains of London's
political and financial forces like a vortex.

Existing context, Vauxhall Cross, London.

This project proposes a giant cross-Thames roundabout, completes the shape already implied by the configuration of the existing roads and turns Vauxhall Cross into Vauxhall Loop. From a cross to a nought, X to O; a speculative urban fantasy, made out of observations, scenarios and proposals that circulate around the area of Vauxhall Cross.

Vauxhall Cross is one of the biggest and most congested traffic interchanges in Central London. It is also a crossroads for conflicting urban forces. In it, political parties and financial institutions, individuals and their local organisations are caught up at the hub of the vortex of change that has taken over London.

Dealing with that dynamic of change, this project uses Henri Lefebvre's *Rhythmanalysis* – a "method of studying an urban situation by the rhythms it produces". In his essay "Seen from the Window" Lefebvre, at his balcony, overlooking a big traffic intersection in Paris, is captured by and tuned to its rhythms. "Attentive to time (or tempo) and therefore as much to repetitions as to differences in time", the author describes the rhythms of traffic as a representation of the workings of the capitalist city.

It is within the rhythms of the city, he claims, that the social order is manifesting itself. This project is to a certain degree a rhythm analysis of Vauxhall Cross – it takes the technique as its starting point and the metaphor of the traffic light as its structure. Red episodes, yellow episodes and green episodes alternate with one another in a repetitive succession, referring to different phases within urban time. Consequently, the green episodes are about movement, describing aspects of progress and travel. The yellow episodes are about transition, dealing with moments of urban change, and

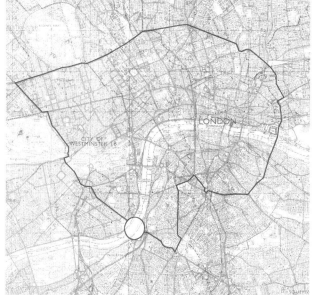

↑↑The node that is Vauxhall Cross is
formed by six feeder roads: Vauxhall
Bridge, Albert Embankment, Kennington Road,
Lambeth Place, Bondway and Wandsworth Road.

↑Central London as defined by the London
Underground Zone 1 with relative size and
location of Vauxhall Nought indicated.

the red ones are about waiting, in which the very
practice of waiting, produced by the rhythms of the
city, is examined for its social and financial
potentials.

Each episode is to a certain degree independent, but
as the narrative unfolds, episodes synchronise and
principles that apply in one field and to certain
organisations are applied to others. The data –
statistical, financial and legal, factual or fictional –
that is woven through the project is a narrative device
in a story conceived out of economics and urban
politics. In these mundane details of the everyday, the
mysteries of urban life emerge. The project takes
capitalist mechanisms for a series of interpretations
and manipulation, it analyses the site in time, and the
social orders as they manifest themselves in it.

If in *Rhythmanalysis* the metaphor of the traffic light
stands for a system of regulation control, the project
proceeds by contrasting this order with a system of
flow. The proposal for the replacement of the traffic
light system with the cross-Thames roundabout liberates
and channels the rhythms of the site into a void flow.

The roundabout alters temporal, political and financial
conditions: it generates 'urban tier' reducing traffic
delay, and in its very configuration it changes legal
and political definitions within its boundary.
A speculative and financial scheme that makes use of
these conditions offers a new urban mechanism capable
of examining future scenarios at a time of approaching
urban change.

GATE
TWO

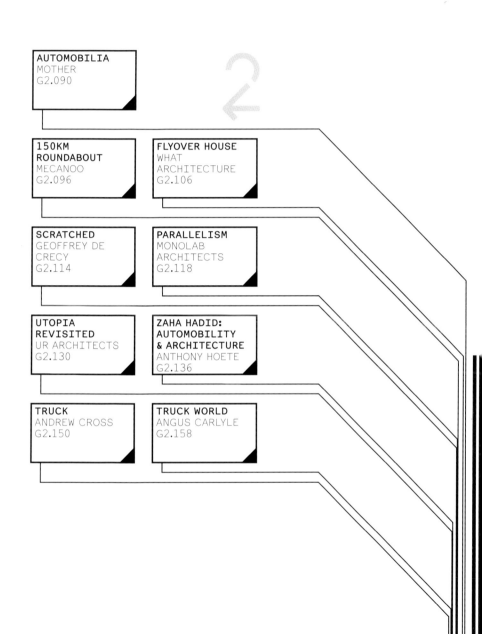

AUTOMOBILIA
MOTHER
G2.090

150KM
ROUNDABOUT
MECANOO
G2.096

FLYOVER HOUSE
WHAT
ARCHITECTURE
G2.106

SCRATCHED
GEOFFREY DE
CRECY
G2.114

PARALLELISM
MONOLAB
ARCHITECTS
G2.118

UTOPIA
REVISITED
UR ARCHITECTS
G2.130

ZAHA HADID:
AUTOMOBILITY
& ARCHITECTURE
ANTHONY HOETE
G2.136

TRUCK
ANDREW CROSS
G2.150

TRUCK WORLD
ANGUS CARLYLE
G2.158

GATE 2:
ON THE ROAD
G2.086

on the road

According to the economist Colin Clark, transport, or the lack of it, is the primary constraint on the size and growth of cities.[1] Prior to the industrialised era of mechanically propelled transportation, horse drawn coaches and boats were the only alternatives to walking: "no citizen of ancient Rome would have been overwhelmed by the scale or pace of eighteenth century London".[2] The absence of any motorised modes limited the city boundaries to the distance its citizens could cover in one hour.

1 Clark, Colin, "Transport Maker and Breaker of Cities", Town Planning Review 28, 1957.

2 Brandon, Ruth, Automobilia, London: Macmillan, 2002, p 130.

With the arrival of the railways this barrier to urban growth was finally overcome. Trains could now carry food into the centre: Farringdon Station, which opened in London in 1863, was part of the world's first underground railway, connecting the countryside to a city abattoir. Cities exploded in both size and population. Paris grew from 550,000 people in 1800 to 2,500,000 by 1900. Over the same period London grew from 860,000 to 4,400,000.[3] As new transportation infrastructures were laid down, new contexts for urban living appeared.

Living adjacent to, beneath or above highways, railway lines and flight paths is today symptomatic of the modern city. The effects on living standards have been less than desirable due to the environmental problems of noise and pollution. Yet the spatio-economic potential of these apparently blighted sites is slowly being recognised: highly accessible and relatively cheap. Interstitial leftover spaces between the city and its infrastructure are undergoing renewed scrutiny in a search for more efficient usage.

More than any other form of transportation, the automobile is the *modus operandi* that shaped the modern city. The city of Los Angeles, for example, is well-recognised as *the* city of asphalt: the surface area of its street network, 1,040km², surpasses that of its inner city area, 880 km².[4] The terrain of the modern city is one of junctions, bypasses, cul-de-sacs, roundabouts and flyovers. The photographs of Andrew Cross, with accompanying text by Angus Carlyle, explore this urban landscape by looking at the world of the truck.

The car determines one potent understanding of the city. In order for this to be appreciated, ROAM explores sites of auto-intensification. The Netherlands has both a high population density – 465 persons per square

3 Brandon, Automobilia.

4 Kenworthy, Jeffrey and Laube, Felix, An International Sourcebook of Automobile Dependence in Cities 1960-1990, Colorado: University Press of Colorado, 1999; www.scag.ca.gov.

kilometre) — as well as high car motorisation — 406 passenger cars per 1000 inhabitants in 2000) — and so a number of Dutch design projects are featured.[6] The Dutch architectural collective, Monolab, consider the concept of 'no man's land', where the *peripherique* and the adjacent *terrain vague* are vacuous spaces awaiting functional realignment: residential space, for example, to be installed within residual space. In UR Architect's "Utopia Revisited", highway intersects with house: a road passes over a 'hump' of residential accommodation. The geometry of this middle-of-the-road construction — the housing is no wider than the road itself — causes traffic to slow facilitating easier vehicular access to one's front door, with the aesthetic suggesting an over-scaled 'sleeping policeman'.

Roads connect nodes in the project *Rings and Roundabout*, a 90 minute road movie converted into radial maps by Mecanoo. The drive by shooting of Europe's busiest 'roadsite' is recorded in 'car-cam' (four video cameras were centrally mounted in a car to capture front, rear and side views), depicting four cities and their connecting 'ringroadscape'. From a 'vroom with a rue' to a room with a view, this section of ROAM moves to the mobile space of the taxi, the setting for a conversation with architect Zaha Hadid.

6 www.planetholiday. com/europe/General/ Netherlands/ Netherlands_general. asp; www.europa.eu. int.

automobilia
mother

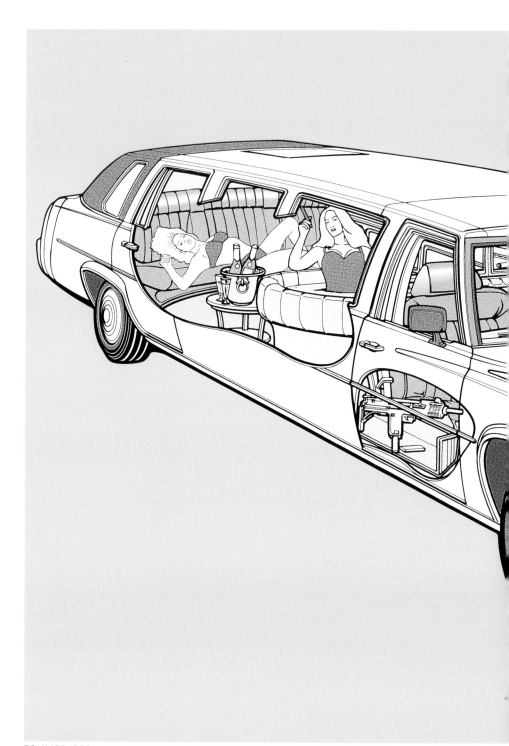

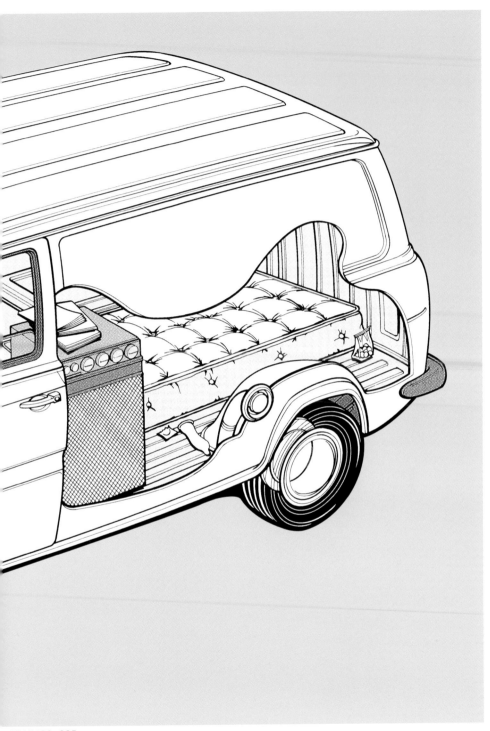

150km
roundabout
mecanoo

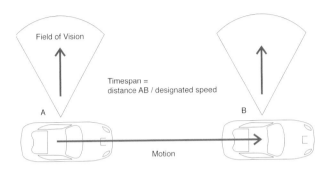

Field of Vision

Timespan =
distance AB / designated speed

A

B

Motion

Such panoramas are filmic in the sense that the filed scenography unfolds without 'zooming in'. The road user experience is akin to the 'tracking shot' common to cinematography. The timespan of the 'tracking shot' is vital for the experience of an open panorama. This is reliant on the speed of the vehicle and the distance travelled. At the high speed of a motorway the length of the panorama therefore needs to be long.

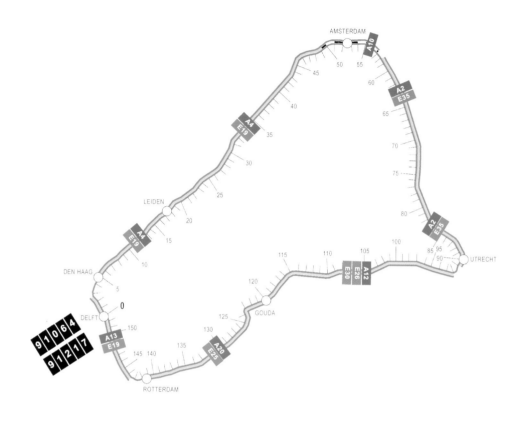

Radial Map 1: The four principle Dutch cities of The Hague, Amsterdam, Utrecht and
Rotterdam form a city state known as the Randstad or Rim City. These 'million town'
cities with relatively small populations of around one million or less form a sum
greater than their parts: an 'uber-urbanism' representing 42% of the national
population. The Randstad is connected by several motorways including the A13, A4, A10,
A2, A12 and the A20 to form a 'metro-loop', the site of investigation for this project.

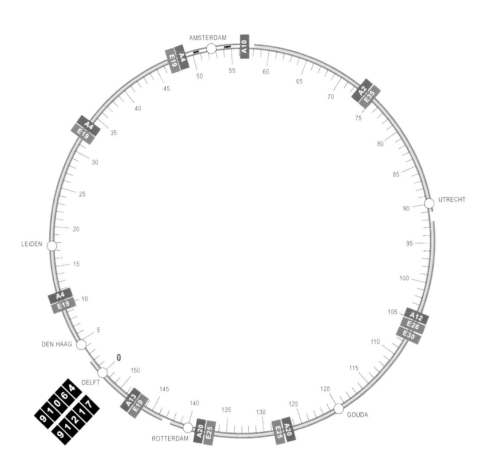

Radial Map 2: The roads that connect the metropoles of the Randstad are conceptualised to form one gigantic roundabout, 150km in circumference, and represented as an odometer for observational clarity.

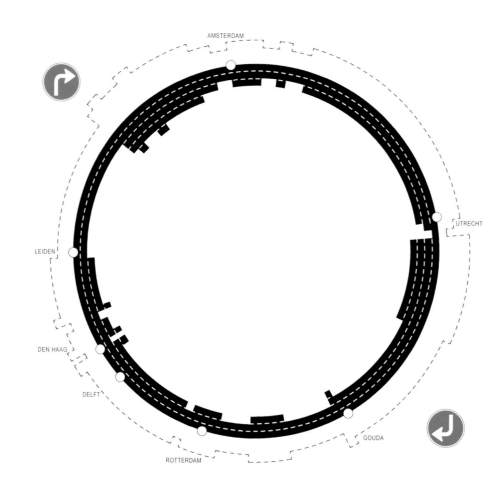

Radial Map 3: The number of lanes that form a highway at any given point is one condition that determines its flow capacity. Around this particular Dutch 'metro loop', the relative volume of traffic moving between the four metropoles fluctuates: five lanes appear on the interior (clockwise direction) before Amsterdam as vehicles leave Schiphol Airport. A one-lane potential bottleneck is found south of Utrecht.
At the moment it is not possible to reverse the designated direction of a lane to cater for daily variations such as the scenario of high traffic volumes leaving a city at evening rush hour.

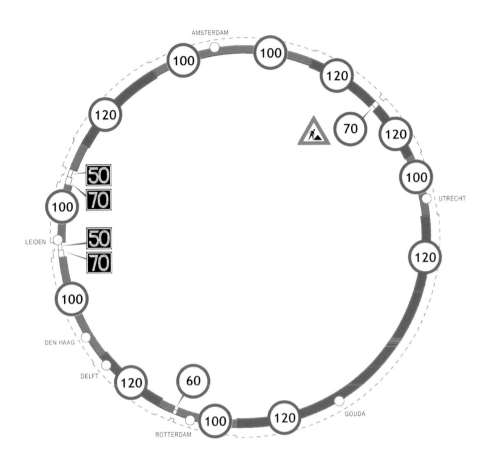

Radial Map 4: The flow rate of the ring road varies according to lane number and the designated speed. Speed has a perceptive consequence on the roaduser's space-time relationship: at slower speeds the level of contextual engagement increase; conversely high speed travel severs the traveller from their surroundings. With the advent of responsive signposting, the speed of the ring road can be regulated around the traffic volume, events (accidents, jams) and roadside programmes.

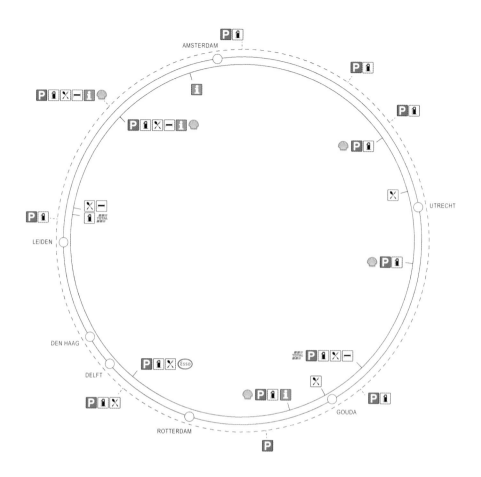

Radial Map 5: Showing the distribution of services and verge programmes around the ring road. Originally petrol stations offered primarily fuel but have since developed into fully fledged service stations with accommodation, restaurant, shopping and transfer facilities. In the future, complementary verge programmes such as swimming pools will appear.

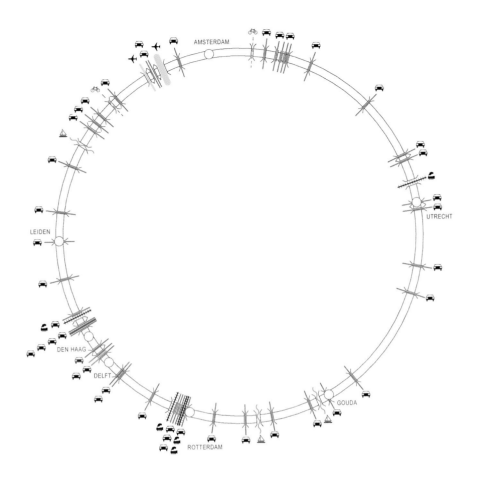

Radial Map 6: One road crosses another either above (flyover), below (underpass, tunnel) or at the same level (intersection). Given the ring road's classification, intersections are not permissable. Around the 153km ring, 57 flyovers were encountered at an average of one flyover every 2.6 km: vehicles (45), trains (5), aqueducts (3), cycles (2) and airport runways (2).

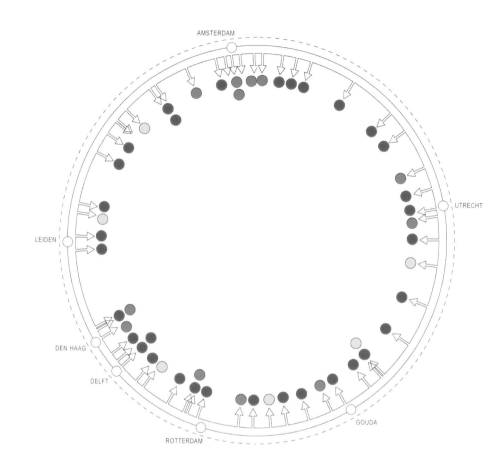

Radial Map 7: 54 offramps fed into the interior of the roundabout meaning an offramp
every 1.7 minutes (at the maximum permissable speed of 100kph). The offramps were
classified according to access programmes. Terminus offramps, shown in red, indicate
destination-based uses such as home or work. Transition offramps, in yellow, indicate
points where one temporarily leaves the ring road for service functions such as petrol
stations and refreshments. Finally, interchange offramps (in green) provide access and
connectivity to other roads.

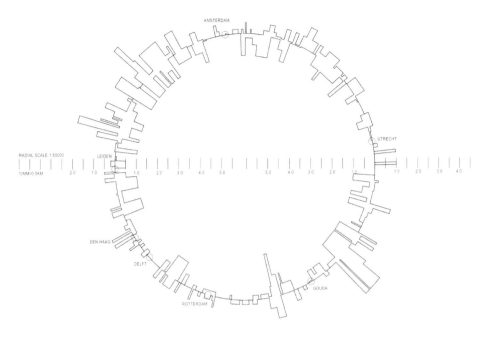

Radial Map 8: In photography, depth of field is a term indicating the distance range
from the focal plane in which objects remain in focus. Depth of field here refers to a
measure of the relative enclosure of the visible landscape through which the road
passes. Looking perpendicularly from the road, two side-view cameras recorded the
obstructed horizon. How far one could see determined the depth of the landscape: deep
fields are less common in cities.

flyover
house
what
architecture

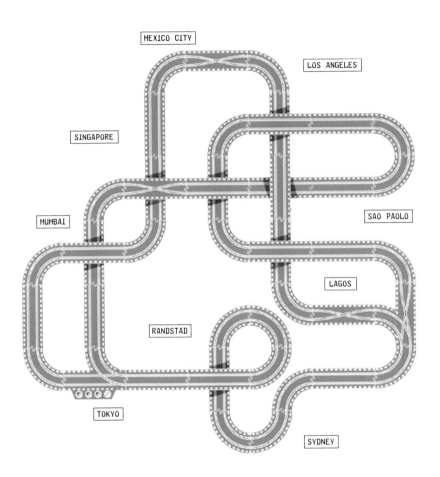

MEXICO CITY

LOS ANGELES

SINGAPORE

MUMBAI

SAO PAOLO

LAGOS

RANDSTAD

TOKYO

SYDNEY

THE ROAD TO KNOW WHERE®

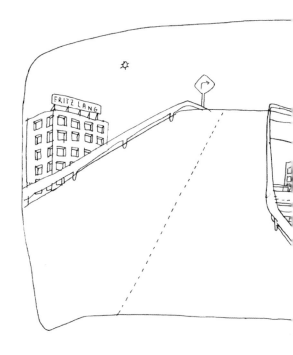

←←The architecture of the today's road is one which has become increasingly standardised for reasons of safety and recognition. Furthemore, with the rise of permissable speeds (Italy's Autostrada and Germany's Autobahnen are almost limitless) the road is today a generic condition, paradoxically connecting places yet disconnecting the roaduser from his or her immediate location: the intracity landscape.

↑The surface of the road is no longer ground bound. The increasing need to verticalise street and road networks due to space-saving developmental pressures in cities leads one to the scenario of 'highrise highways'.

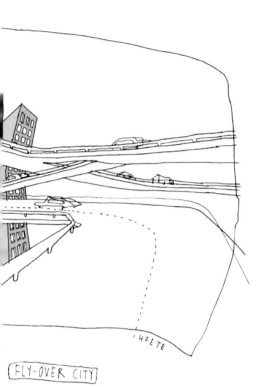

HOETE

FLY-OVER CITY

The Flyover House is an artificial site that
accommodates a small car-dependent commuter community.
To counter the noise and asphalt aesthetic, landscaping
and planting form hedges, a vegetative threshold, so
that, from inside your home, the road disappears from
view. Being a hybrid, some of the qualities particular
to a bridge – such as linearity – are deliberately
foresaken in favour of a square plane of increased
social interactivity – less a strip Ponte Vecchio than
an elevated Albert Square. The flyover house occupies no
more space than the road below: in so doing it
simultaneously offers the road below a stimulating

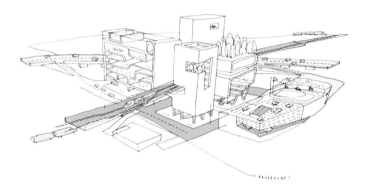

The city of the future will function as a
place of interchange and intersection.
Architecture will lie at the crossroads of
modal connectivity.

drive-through experience – the tunnel is a shadowy
portal that is driven through the landscape. Dark space
is problematic for architecture which revels in the
"play of light upon form and mass" yet is less
problematic for the motorist as it provides temporary
visual stimulus from the fatigue of driving. Street
signs are replaced by road signs and one's house is
accessed directly via an off-ramp. Highway architecture:
no middle-of-the-road building!

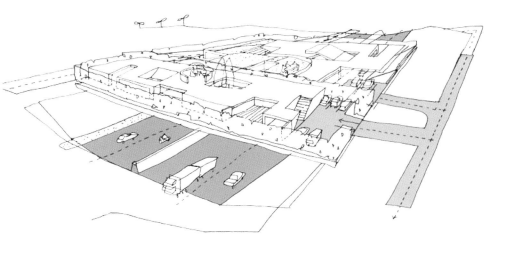

Infrastructural architectures demand
that transportational lines develop verge
programmes other than those which are
purely commercial. Roadside residences
such as the Flyover House offer high
levels of accessibility and install
suburban qualities within urban densities.
Hedge conditions filter out unwanted
views, sounds and smells.

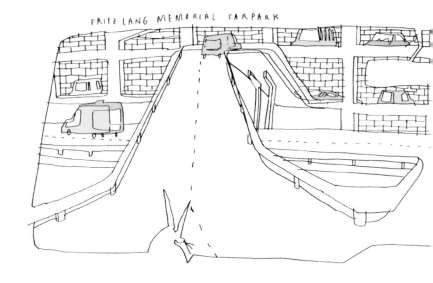

FRITZ LANG MEMORIAL CARPARK

15 STOREYS

TO 5TH AVENUE

HOETE

CITY PARKING

ROM HIGHWAY

Much has been made of the car's invasion
of the metropolis. As the city infills
and rises, scenic drives will no longer
feature natural landscapes but urban
scenographies: auto-elevators, sky bridges
between buildings, observation decks and
parking plateaus.

scratched
geoffrey de crecy

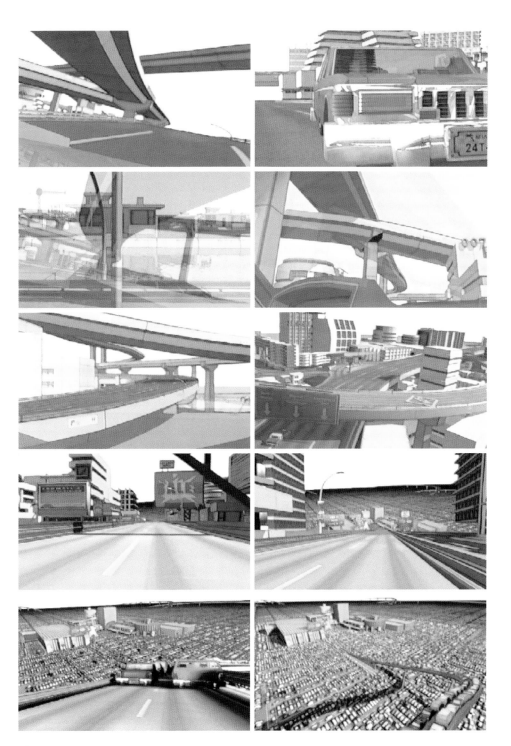

parallelism
monolab

Three main issues trigger the projects of Monolab: infrastructure, density and landscape. The numb attitude of Dutch governance since the 1980s has caused three devastating crises in spatial planning:

1. infrastructure and its spin-off have been neglected.

2. a proliferation of low-density suburbanism has invaded large parts of the country.

3. its consensus society created a swamp of laws and regulations, suffocating urbanism and architecture by short-term political agendas.

←←View into the project Leidsche Rijn which creates a vehicle free city centre for the largest 'Vinex' location in the Netherlands through an infrastructural breeder sheet.

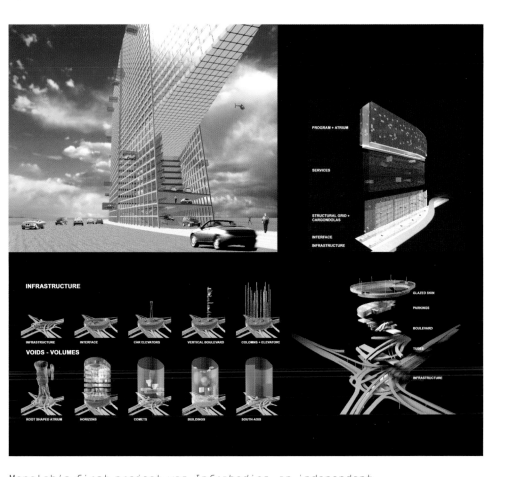

Monolab's first project was *Infrabodies*, an independent case study for Rotterdam into the programming of urban vacuums, empty zones along heavy infrastructure. All aspects of infrastructure were approached with a 'positive attitude', creating a fusion between all programmatic parts. A new way of working was projected by turning so-called problems into chances, opportunities and new ideas. *Infrabodies* resulted in four commissions.

As an alternative to the point development and intensification of infrastructural nodes, sites along the road ('roadsites') offer further spatial economic opportunities.

The 'stacking' of programmes in order to yield higher site densities is a prominent feature of contemporary Dutch architecture (Koolhaas et al). This spatial strategy is the pragmatic coupling of a high population density (320 persons per square kilometre), and thus limited ground space, to an economic means.

The first was *Delft South Station*, for the city of Delft,
the site being a nodal point of highway and train
tracks, obstructing four city quarters. The design
linked highway, public transport, local traffic,
station, bicycle highway, city quarters, etc.. The
station was excavated in a booster – a programme on top
of the site – triggering its development. This booster
should fit any programme, designed as a dense structural
system that branches into a limited number of
structural members between the tracks.

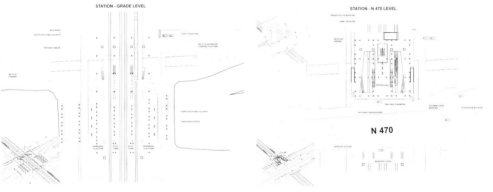

STATION - GRADE LEVEL

STATION - N 470 LEVEL

N 470

For the second project, *Compressor*, for the Ministry of Spatial Planning, we looked past the present to 2030. The issue of the post-Vinex-question (low-density residential projects behaving as parasites on towns and cities) evoked an 'exponential urbanism' by the projection of a sheer mass (2.3 million m² floorspace) on an infrastructural nodal point.[1] The problem was how to make this mass liveable (admittance of light and air) and how to tilt horizontal infrastructural systems towards the vertical. Slabs of city were stacked, with each slab having its own soil on top, as part of an extensive atrium system.

1 Vinex, or Vierde Nota Ruimtelijke Ordening Extra, is the Fourth Note on Extra Spatial Planning announced by the Dutch Ministry of Housing, Spatial Planning and the Environment (VROM). This spatio-political masterplan for an entire nation (albeit Europe's most densely populated) specifies a number of 'Vinex-locations' in which residential areas will be intensely developed as urban extensions. These locations are often detached from existing lines of infrastructure. For a complete list of all the Vinex locations, visit www.vinex-locaties.nl.

The seamless transition from car to house in Compressor is made possible by the verticalised programming of the roundabout.

→Infrastructure has a prominence that surpasses that of architecture: roads consume large tracts of land and demand long-term political commitment. The construction cost, for example of a two-lane Dutch highway is around €1 million per kilometre with a land reservation 50 metres wide.

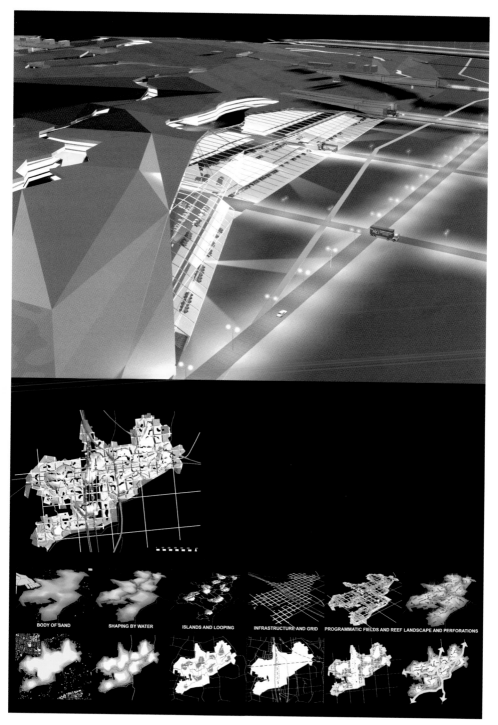

BODY OF SAND   SHAPING BY WATER   ISLANDS AND LOOPING   INFRASTRUCTURE AND GRID   PROGRAMMATIC FIELDS AND REEF LANDSCAPE AND PERFORATIONS

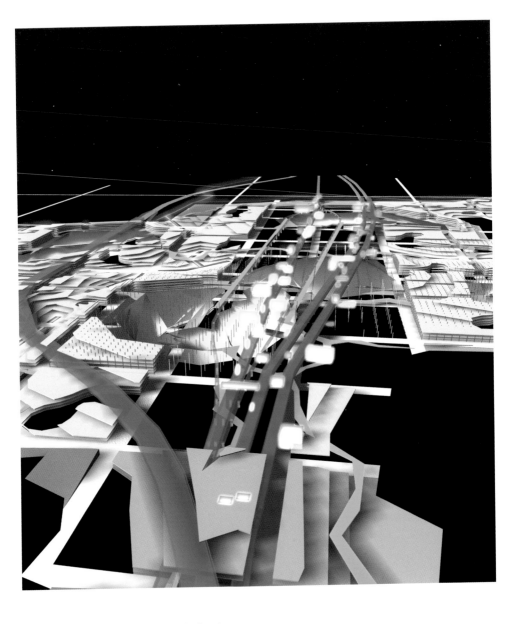

Projected view: Infrascape Breda Sands.

The third project *Infrascape Breda Sands*, for the
Province of Noord Brabant, is a design for a high speed
train station (HST) between Amsterdam-Schiphol and
Brussels-Zaventem, a station for trains that would not
stop in Brabant.

The Province of Brabant is only one of a few government
bodies in Holland that is clearly alarmed by the
increase of urban sprawl. Lack of urban control by a
backseat government and a subsequent overflow of the
'Randstad', causes a haze of built material resulting in
an absence of defined landscape and cities, creating a
blurring 'urban vague'. In an attempt to create a
'hidden' urbanism, the design was submerged into
landscape. A huge body of sand, shaped by rediscovered
streams, was used to transmit the landscape over infra-
barriers. Excavations, create a grid on ground level,
with a circuit for pedestrians/cyclists on the first
level, infrastructural tubes for freeway and highway
and HST on the second level, resulting in a landscape on
top. Brabant's small ponds were translated into atriums,
perforating the landscape and fields. The landscape
itself almost acted as a skin, by separating and
connecting completely different worlds.

The scheme for the fourth project *City Center Leidsche Rijn*, for the city of Utrecht, creates a vehicle free city centre for the 80,000 new inhabitants of Leidsche Rijn, the largest Vinex in Holland. It adds one third of the present number of inhabitants of the city of Utrecht on top of an infrastructural node: a crossing of A2 highway, train tracks and city road. The infernal conditions of the A2 highway (10 lanes in a total width of 80 m.) were restrained by integration and absorption. The vehicle free context was realised by an infrastructural 'breeder sheet' that facilitates a complete accessibility for inhabitants, visitors, large-scale commercial programme, delivery, transfer, parking and public transport. The city floor, hovering over these services, is free of vehicles and negative conditions of delivery and public transport. This floor creates an eco-system for pedestrians.

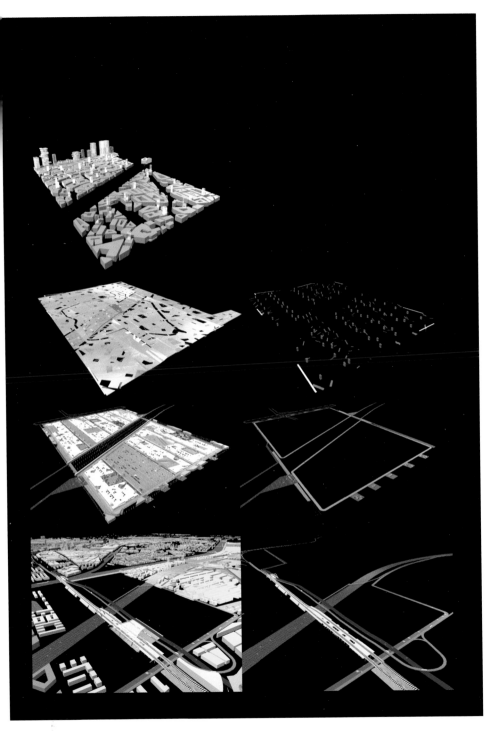

utopia
revisited
ur
architects

A 'polder' is an artificial land,
typically open and broad,
reclaimed from the sea and thus
lying below sea level. In Lelystad,
the Netherlands, the polder
has been lost, hidden within the
layers of the city. There is a
contradiction of scale and
aspiration: the city centre is too
small, the infrastructure too big.
Miniature highways connect to
suburbia and bridges plunge into
vast slow traffic areas filled with
fragmented two storey dwellings.
However, within the larger
provincial scale of Flevoland
there is potential for Lelystad.
Just a few metres above the
artificial horizon of suburban
housing, you can start to survey
the polder, become aware of its
openness, beyond suburbia, beyond
the boundaries of the immediate
urban environment.

←←Neighbourhood watch? An overscaled
'sleeping policeman' forms a bump in the
road into which housing is inserted.

The 1990s gave rise to the idea of institutionalised leisure; it became a part of everyday life, a requirement for living, a necessity for everyone. This focus on relaxation is reflected in Lelystad, with the spatial dynamics of the new waterfront developments and city centre masterplanning not only adding diversity to the city but also stimulating alternative forms of society to that of the suburban model. Within this context, new forms and sites for housing are being investigated. The unpopulated verge area surrounding the city is one site with easy urban access and low economic value (because of environmental issues), allowing for three possible configurations: above, below and beside the road. A 'new wave' of dwelling, a bridge building, is proposed, passing the highway over what is essentially terraced housing. In lifting the road from its landscape, the environment is not severed but remains continuous, simultaneously giving the flat, open 'polderscape' around Lelystad a landmark. The space around the building becomes a place for the collective assembly of its inhabitants. By driving over this building, the car is elevated allowing a momentary overview of the flat lands. This driving experience – an event – allows the occupants of the car to absorb the landscape before once more descending below the waterline of Lelystad.

This design simultaneously acts as building, infrastructure and landscape. Access by car is possible to all dwellings through the creation of a series of elevated ground floors and, in turn, the houses are afforded panoramas. 70% of the dwellings are ground based with south facing private gardens; the remainder have large south facing terraces and views of the landscape beyond. Two dwelling types have been defined within the proposal, the 'tunnel' rowhouse and the 'patio apartment', both of which have a high degree of

flexibility and adaptability. This diversification of
the dwellings is further enhanced by the specificity of
their location within the whole building - sometimes
garden dwellings and at other times lofts, stacked upon
each other in varying configurations. This stacking is a
concept that continues throughout the whole
organisation of the building, from car to living. The
tunnel rowhouse, which occupies two levels, is linked
through the verge by two walkways. It provides two and
three bedroom dwellings with the possibility of an
extra space in one or more of the car parking spaces. The
patio apartment occupies one level and wraps around a
court within the verge, gives easier access for elderly
and disabled occupants. They have the opportunity of
living on the top floor and still having the car parked
outside their front door! The pragmatics of combining
the various infrastructures continues with the
construction of the building. Damper systems, open
asphalt road and the car speed limited to 50kph all
combine to reduce the transmission of contact noise.

The modern urbanist Cornelius Van Eesteren proposed the
centre of Lelystad to be elevated above the residential
area and connected to the sea. Our design allows the
road to pass over the dwellings of a new suburbia, down
to the sea on an architectural rollercoaster ride.

→↑The 'new wave' of Dutch housing, which
positions the road into, beside, below and
above residential space has the added
advantage of providing a scenic lookout
down onto the otherwise featureless flat
landscape that characterises the
Netherlands.

→↓Two advantages of 'underpass' housing:
road noise is significantly reduced as the
road can be formed to project sound up;
the road no longer severs the landscape as
each house has interrupted landscape access
through a garden.

zaha hadid: automobility and architecture
anthony hoete

Perhaps surprisingly, given the number of mobility projects her office is currently engaged with, Zaha Hadid doesn't drive. She is chauffeured around London in her very own black cab, citing pragmatic reasons for her choice of automobile: the taxi is like a van for carrying models and drawings. It is a machine for working in, a minicab for minicad. Other unannounced benefits include the use of lanes reserved for buses and taxis. The mobile space of the taxi, at once public and private, is a void that renders its mobilised occupants anonymous amongst the humdrum of city traffic and urban flows. Somewhat quixotically, Hadid's other car is a Smart.

A Taxi Driver's Guide to the City

Of the countless citizens whose daily routines have undoubtedly equipped them with an acquired spatial understanding of the city, the taxi driver stands apart. 'The Knowledge' is a formal examination required by licensed black cab drivers, testing their ability to locate any street or public building within London. For example, in the map test "How to become a London Taxi Driver?" one question asks, "Where is the Croatian Embassy?" Such metro processing is no trivial feat given the inherent multiplicity of London's street names: 23 King's Roads and seven Queen Streets. For someone whose automobile existence is solely one as passenger, it is remarkable that Hadid herself professes to know every short cut between her home in Kensington and her office in Clerkenwell. These daily journeys – the city sectioned by the car – reveal how this metropole has metamorphosed in the last few years from 'greasy spoons' to Starbucks.

The reconstitution of the taxi ride as urban pyschogeography *par excellence* is not limited to the dynamics of location and pathfinding; no, the contemporary taxi ride is an event-space incorporating chat room, opinion poll, counsel chamber and meteorological office. The taxi ride as this interiorised public space is also seen disconnected from various urban settings in Jim Jarmusch's film *Night on Earth*. Suspended between fixed destinations, the film circulates around the brief, but poignant, encounters between a driver and his/her passenger over five simultaneous taxi rides: Los Angeles, Rome, Helsinki, Paris and New York.

BMW Plant Leipzig, Germany: the central building is a communication knot, the active nerve centre for the entire factory complex. From here, all threads of the building's activities converge and diverge. This organisational strategy applies not only to the building's occupants but also to the automated production line.

The taxi as publicity machine

The taxi is partly a public space and its surfaces are thus festooned with advertising – Metrocab Advertising declares that by "travelling in close proximity to the advert, in a relaxed atmosphere of modern comfort and privacy, the passenger absorbs your message". That Hadid owns the one automobile that doubles as a mobile billboard is consistent with her media presence. The work of Zaha Hadid, however, is its own advert and through it she has become one of the world's most *visible* architect. Her obsessive preoccupation with the formal qualities of architecture renders an aesthetic vocabulary that is at once recognisable and instantly legible. This is an indictment of the globalisation of architecture as brand building where the super-client is free to pick'n'mix from the architectural supermarket. Few architects have controlled, developed, formed and articulated architecture through its visual media (painting, drawing, modelling, building) like Hadid has done. The product is unquestionable identity and authorship. The anonymity of the architectural competition is laughable when confronted by an *oeuvre* whose signature lies not as a logo-in-the-corner but in the iconic composition of the work itself. Such formal pursuits have also afforded Hadid's greatest criticism. Her first built project, the Vitra Fire Station in Weil am Rhein, Germany, engaged with movement through purely sculptural manipulations. 'Dynamic' fragments and shards mark the appearance of this project, but these are the by-products or after-effects of her aversion towards orthogonal geometry. The building thus looks like a photograph of an explosion rather than the explosion itself: any motion is merely implied rather than actual.

Ground floor plan of BMW project, Leipzig:
the point of confluence and culmination
for the various production flows.

The value of this work is that it shows architecture in stasis. Architecture's appreciation of mobility in the modernist period was in its aesthetic expression. Buildings aspired to look like boats and cars. Movement in buildings was a caricature of the 'dynamic', undertaken as the formal pursuit of composition. If architecture continues to be imagined as 'still life' then it will always remain pedestrian.

Having established the scene, we now direct discussions towards Hadid's own brand of carchitecture. As a perpetual passenger Hadid's own architectural vision is characterised by a sense of motion and her work is permeated with intersecting paths, junctions, routes and vectors. Highway engineering and bridge building have been deployed as internal mechanisms to organise space; "the interesting thing about motorways and intersections is how they bundle and separate, come together again and separate". This interest is prominent in Hadid's recent winning entry for the BMW competition for an Administrative Building in Leipzig. Here the Central Building is the active nerve-centre, or brain, of the factory complex. All threads of the building's activities converge, intersect and diverge from this

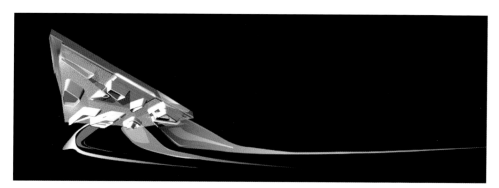

Science Centre, Wolfsburg.

focal point. The organisational strategy here applies to the routine and trajectories of the employees as well as for the cycle and procedures of the production line. It appears as if the entire expanse of this side of the factory is oriented and animated by a force field emanating from the Central Building. All movement converging on the site is funnelled through this compression chamber squeezed in-between the three main segments of production: 'Body in White', Paint Shop and Assembly.

Popular Mechanics

The primary organisational strategy is formalised as a scissor-section connecting ground floor and first floor as a continuous field. Two sequences of terraced plates — like giant staircases — step up from north to south and vice versa. One commences close to the public lobby passing by and overlooking the forum to reach the first floor in the middle of the building. The other cascade starts with the cafeteria at the south end moving up to meet the first floor before proceeding all the way up to the space projecting over the entry. The two cascading sequences capture a long connective void between them. At the bottom of this void is the auditing foyer — the centre of attention

Landesgartenschau, Weil Am Rhein.

for the production plant. Overhead, half-finished cars move along a production line. The cascading floor plates are large enough to allow for reconfigurable occupation patterns, promoting greater visual dialogue than permissible on a single floor plate.

Car production plants have a history of establishing new employment conditions. For instance, Henry Ford, who introduced the production line technique of repetitive specialist tasks, compensated for the tedium by offering minimum wages and employee housing to his workers. With the threat of union action ever looming, the mixing of blue and white collar workers is crucial for the prolonged success of BMW. The architectural means for political accountability is once again spatial transparency, and so a high level of visibility is provided between managerial and production departments. The mixing of functions further avoids the traditional segregation into status groups that is no longer conducive in the modern workplace.

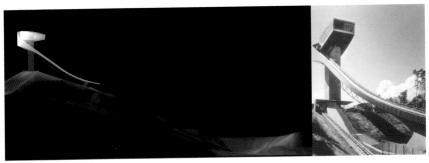

The Bergisel Mountain Ski Jump overlooks Innsbruck (Austria) and replaces the former ski jump which no longer meets international standards. The building is a hybrid of a specialised sporting and public catering facilities (café and observation deck). The two programmes are intertwined into a single form, which extends the natural topography of the mountain slope into the sky.

Standing at a height of 50m and with a length of 90m, the building is a typological combination of a tower and a ramp.

Infrascapes

The scalar range of architecture is shifting. Until recently architecture was preoccupied with scales of space that were more often than not building fixated. One could conveniently describe this as operating between scale 1:20 and 1:200. Today, infrastructure and landscape, 'infrascapes', have increasingly become the new design scales for architecture. The Carpark and Terminus Hoenheim-Nord, commissioned by the city of Strasbourg, is just such a project, with its concept of overlapping fields and lines, knitting together to form a constantly shifting whole. The fields are the patterns of movement engendered by cars, trams, bicycles and pedestrians. Each has a trajectory and a trace as well as being a static fixture. The transition between modal types is seemingly materialised in the station, landscaping and its context. The Carpark is divided into two parts catering for 700 vehicles. The notion of the cars as being ephemeral and constantly changing elements on site is manifest as a 'magnetic field' of white lines on the black tarmac. Each parking space is orientated North/South at one end of the site. Each subsequent row is then rotated one degree causing the entire Carpark composition to twist. Each parking space is identified with a vertical light post and these collectively establish an artificial datum against the varying topography. In contrast with the ground lines, a zone of dark concrete, an imaginary shadow – reminiscent of the Bolles Wilson's Ninja shadow on the façade of their Suzuki house – slices like a sinister presence through the Carpark.

The city of Strasbourg has been developing its tram service to combat increasing congestion and pollution. Through 'park and ride' projects, specific locations provide inter-modal transfer points with which to access the city centre. The planning of the Carpark and Station Terminus at Hoenhiem North overlaps lines and fields of movement to form a constantly shifting whole.

Carpark and Station Terminus, Hoenhiem
North, Strasbourg.

ROAM/G2.148

Urban taxidermy

Urban taxidermy is the architecture of organising, arranging and programming the city in order to give it the appearance of vitality. Are the presence of cabs and taxis enough to suggest a bustling metropolis? Hadid recognises the strained relationship between the automobile and the city through her daily commutes. London is, after all, a city so heavily congested by poor transport planning that the average speed of traffic at the beginning of the twentieth century was no greater than that at the beginning of the twenty-first. If the city of speed is the city of success, as Le Corbusier proclaimed, then London is a resounding failure. Yet our experience of any city, and hence our response to architecture, remains one that is almost exclusively conducted through the space of the automobile. No longer just a means of getting from A to B, the journey is a place to be. The automobile has been an integral part of metropolitan life for so long that it is part of the urban fabric. That the taxi journey has overtaken that of the car is down to its urban engagement: a mobile public-private space, a city icon (the black cabs of London, the yellow cabs of NYC, the white taxis of Sydney, the Ambassadors of Bombay) and at times an urban cinema with its show of speed, event, movement and accompanying driver-narration.

truck world

angus carlyle

We are familiar with the `Zenning` of the motorcycle articulated by Robert M Pirsig. There are the hymns to the muscular momentum of the train sung by the Italian Futurists, with backing tracks performed by Kraftwerk. The celebration of the airplane emerges with lyrical energy from the notebooks of Le Corbusier and the writings of Saint-Exupery. The notion of the car simultaneously emerges as a mechanism for isolated existential agonising and for collective communication/communion. It is commemorated by Jack Kerouac and condemned by J G Ballard. Even nautical vessels have had their enthusiasts, revealed as much in the ship's incorporation into Art Deco aesthetics and modernist architecture as in the more rudimentary boat's persistence as a literary and cinematic device to encapsulate the purported conflict between the individual and "the elements". The truck, however, does not yet seem to have acquired the elevated aura that has been attached to alternative forms of transport.

This is not to say that the truck is bereft of imaginative association, rather that the associations it attracts have rarely scaled the rarefied heights to which other vehicles have ascended. In the early 1970s, numerous popular songs and films celebrated the truck as a symbol both of a certain bearded sexual liberty and of a blue collar middle-fingering to government. Yet not all explorations of trucks and trucking have conformed to an ideal of heterosexual resistance to authority, and memorable exceptions can be found. The autobiography of black science fiction author Samuel R Delany turns the moving rig and static trailer of the long-distance lorry into perverse spaces of spontaneous sexual encounters far removed from Kris Kristofferson's shampooed locks. Moreover, the strange cinematic enterprises *Duel* and *Trucks*, both of which orchestrate their narratives around the pursuit of humans by apparently autonomous lorries, indicate the cultural traffic is not all travelling in the direction of an ode to the truck.

Nevertheless, the correlation between trucks and narrowly defined sexual and political freedom resonated through the 1970s and into the 80s with sufficient volume for the English satirical series *Not the Nine O'Clock News* to offer the world their song "I Like Trucking and I Like to Truck" in 1984. Indeed, this notion of trucking persisted in the regular Truck Fests held throughout Europe, complete with country-rock stages and the fiercely competitive ranking of the airbrushed exteriors of lorry cabs and trailers, the designs of which evoked a limited repertoire of Americana imagery. Away from the world of 'glamour trucking', a political dimension has been maintained with European haulage drivers – particularly French and English – engaging in various demonstrations against perceived threats to their professional survival.

Having spent some time talking to truck drivers about their experiences, it becomes clear that irrespective of the coherence of any concerns relating to fuel taxation, theirs is by no means the carefree existence that the vernacular representations of trucking imply; despite — and sometimes paradoxically because of — European Union directives that impose rigorous parameters on the working day, the truck driver's routine is an extraordinarily arduous one. According to my interviewees, weeks when the driver is away from home from between four and five days are typical, a factor which provoked one driver to declare that this was "only really a job for loners...". The period spent travelling is one in which the drivers are prone to a variety of ailments from acute boredom, through prolonged stress to potentially serious lumbar problems (these latter inspiring the purchase of Scholl back massagers that can be connected to the cab's cigarette lighter when the driver's employers have not already supplied such a device). The onerous working day, which routinely extends from driving to completing paperwork and discharging responsibilities for loading and unloading stock, is exacerbated to the extent that it is conducted under the scrutiny of various forms of surveillance: the tachometer that provides a diagram of the journey's speeds and stops and is audited externally with the results being fed back to the drivers employers and, potentially, the transport regulators; the monitoring of various aspects of vehicle safety; and the customs police endeavouring to thwart the smuggling of goods and people that may have surreptitiously found their way into the trailer. Should any individuals defined by the British press and government in the offensive language of "illegal immigrants" actually manage to circumvent the carbon dioxide checks conducted in Calais and stow on board a truck to the UK, the driver

will be liable for a £2,000 civil penalty if he or she
was unaware of their presence and criminal sanctions
if he or she was. It is not, however, only the
intervention of official bodies about which the
drivers need to display vigilance. The value of the
goods being transported (one driver I talked to
regularly ran loads in excess of £250,000) meant that
trucks were additionally subject to illicit
attentions. "If you park up in a lay-by, you can
guarantee that when you wake up in the morning your
[trailer] curtains will have been cut". That many of
the contracted British lorry drivers I spoke with were
either on or just above the national minimum wage,
necessitating that their income needed to be
supplemented by overtime, determined that the
cumulative pressures of the job were in no way
alleviated by financial compensation.

As Paul Virillo announced in *The Aesthetics of
Disappearance*, "to go nowhere, even to ride around in a
deserted quarter or in a crowded freeway, now seems
natural" and it is tempting to portray the lorry
driver travelling on just such a road to nowhere; to
see the driver as a romantic nihilist-nomad with
"neither hearth nor home" and nothing to lose. There
are those who have succumbed to such a temptation and
have, like Robert Harbison in *Eccentric Spaces*,
declared that "roads progress towards the conceptual,
and faster roads smooth out the scenery; borders of
interstate highways are regularised, perhaps an
epitome of what all roads strive for – to be nowhere,
only to be going". Yet from my perspective, such an
interpretation simply does not ring true of the
stories recounted to me by the drivers I encountered.
Rather than travelling to nowhere, the drivers had
already in a sense arrived since rather than being
dislocated from domesticity, they had laboured to

establish a surrogate habitat within their own cabs. "It is more or less like living in your own house... a real mobile home". The cabs I explored were replete with a variety of creature comforts – comfortable beds, fridges, televisions, CB radios, microwaves, convection cookers, blinds, wardrobes and other storage 'cubbies' – and were isolated from the ground by their elevation and from the environment by their powerful air-conditioning, heating and noise-reduction systems. However, although homes in almost every functional sense, the cabs were rarely 'homey' in the sense of exuding an individualised comfort. Rather than being confronted by swathes of pornographic material that my condescending conscience had anticipated, the most ribald images on display involved pages of stylised lorry photographs removed from issues of *Trucking International* or *Truck and Driver*. This absence of overt customisation was explained as a regrettable consequence of my interviewees' status as contracted employees who therefore possessed none of the decorative independence afforded to the owner-drivers, who were free to ornament their vehicular space according to their own imaginations. Nevertheless, a subdued and transient personalisation was occasionally affected in the cabs: a posed photograph temporarily attached to the sun visor, a commemorative ashtray velcroed to the dashboard (and thus able to be removed upon arrival at the depot), a football scarf discretely folded on top of a spare set of overalls.

Perhaps such subtle encroachments into the sterile space of a confined compartment amount to a precursor of a future definition of 'home' from which our contemporary accommodation will appear redundantly baroque in comparison. For the moment, however, let us indulge in another interpretation of the truck, one that accords it the prestige other transportation has already secured and let us rework Roland Barthes' meditations on the ship in *Mythologies* into a meditation on the truck:

An inclination for [trucks] always means the joy of perfectly enclosing oneself, of having at hand the greatest possible number of objects, and having at one's disposal an absolutely infinite space. To like [trucks] is first and foremost to like a house which is absolutely perfect on account of its unremitting enclosure, and not at all to like vague voyages into the unknown: a [truck] is something that you live in rather than something that you travel in.

GATE
THREE

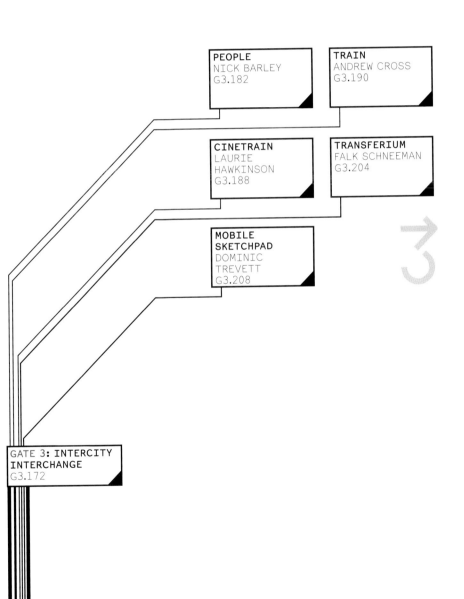

PEOPLE
NICK BARLEY
G3.182

TRAIN
ANDREW CROSS
G3.190

CINETRAIN
LAURIE
HAWKINSON
G3.188

TRANSFERIUM
FALK SCHNEEMAN
G3.204

**MOBILE
SKETCHPAD**
DOMINIC
TREVETT
G3.208

GATE 3: INTERCITY
INTERCHANGE
G3.172

intercity
interchange

The following section of ROAM moves from the motorway to the railway and the runway. The railroad, bringing food and raw material in and carrying finished goods out of the urban centre, was the first mechanically powered mode to enable the population of a city to grow rapidly. Population growth was not, however, accompanied by a ground area expansion, for whilst the installation of railroads allowed more people and goods to be moved in, the city still lacked an internal means of transportation. Population densities of city centres thus increased dramatically: by 1900, immigrants to New York made the city the most crowded in the world with 250,000 inhabitants per square kilometre, 25 times more than New York's population per square kilometre at the end of the twentieth century. [1]

1 Roberts, Gerrylynn K and Philip Steadman, eds, American Cities and Technology, London: Routledge, 1999.

↑↑The Bulgarian Express, Bulgaria.

↑The Jan Pietersz Express,
Germany-Holland.

↑↑The Lisinki Express, Croatia.

↑London-Amsterdam via Harwich.

↑↑The Verdi Express, Italy-Switzerland.
↑The Rhein Sprinter Express, Germany.

↑↑The Rembrandt Express, Switzerland.
↑The Ost-West Express, Germany-Poland.

Today the interconnectivity of rail to road is apparent. As a state improves its rail infrastructure, its dependency on the automobile decreases. In Western Europe, the development of high speed lines mean that rail networks are covering ever-increasing distances, spatially overlapping with 'short hop' airline networks. Furthermore, Europe is being spatio-temporally reconfigured as cities move towards or drift away from each other along the lines of their connecting infrastructures. Paris, once two days by horse, is now two hours by train – delays pending. A map of "High Speed Europe" shows the current progress of the European high speed rail network and the resulting geographic and spatial distortions in travel time. The value society bestows upon its 'need for speed' demands a consideration of the ecological and economic consequences, as low speed modal lines litter the landscape.[2] The spatial economics of mobility prompt a programmatic recycling of space *and* service, with this multi-functionality yielding unexpected potential – the 'reinvention' of the train brings added value to the rail journey. Laurie Hawkinson's *Cinetrain* transforms the train into a cinematic apparatus for the production and projection of film, playing with the idea of the train journey offering a cinematic experience with scenes animated by the train's movement and framed by the landscapes flattened against the passenger's window. In "Transferium" by Falk Schneemann, the idea of the railway station as a site for transition, change and movement is explored. This architectural proposal, structured vertically, intensifies ground use whilst simultaneously providing a stacked platform/belvedere to the city. The station is thus a place of modal split, a place for changing and transferring one's means of mobility.

2 Hawken, Paul, Amory Lovins and L Hunter Lovins, Natural Capitalism: creating the next industrial revolution, London: Earthspan, 1999.

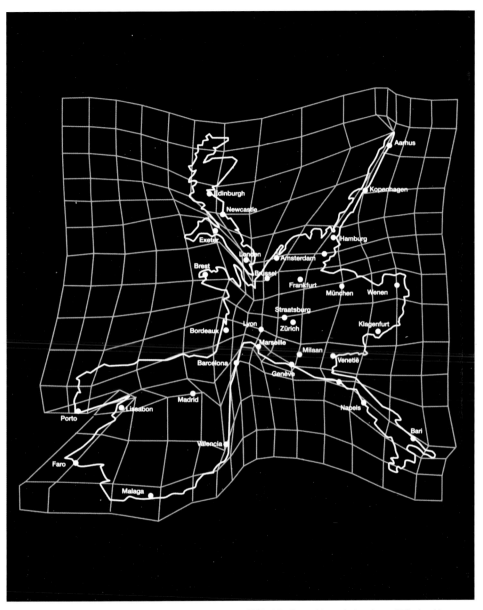

↑Spatio-temporal map indicating the
relative positions of various European
cities. Unlike a conventional map which
charts distance, such a map indicates the
relative location according to travel time.
With the development of the European high
speed rail network (speeds in excess of
300kph) the city of London will in the
future, for example, gravitate by 'moving
closer' (in terms of travel time) to the
dense uber-urbanisms of Northern Europe;
The Randstad, Flanders and the Ruhrgebeit
pulling the United Kingdom apart as this
projection shows.

Similarly, the modern airport is the interchange at its most extreme – its cross-sectional layering of airplane on tarmac, connected by skybridge to terminals of escalators, elevators and travelators, with Departures over Arrivals to taxis, buses and cars, and finally, the subterranean depths of rail connections. Over 100 million passengers a year are welcomed at London's pentangle of major international airports. As Nick Barley's essay "People" observes that the airports of Heathrow, Gatwick, Stanstead, Luton and City are almost the only places that announce you are actually in the shifting location that is London. This uncertainty of urban identity is exemplified in the geographic distortion that city re-branding has brought about. At Luton, base for the budget airline EasyJet, the commercial pressures generated by its airport have mutated two cities, separated by 50km, into one: arrivals are greeted with the ambiguity of "Welcome to London Luton". This tendency towards 'urban impersonation' is the result of low cost airlines seeking out cheaper landing slots in places that approximate destinations. The cases of the Belgian airport of Brussels South, a destination that actually lies in Charleroi 75km further south of Brussels, and the German Airport Frankfurt Hahn, which is actually closer to Luxembourg (110km) than Frankfurt centre (125km), are two of numerous examples of 'aircity' mutation – exercises in mobility for economic, rather than conceptual reasons.[3]

3 www.world airportguide.com.

European high speed rail networks.

people
nick
barley

Every city-dweller is familiar with the experience of inching forwards in an interminable traffic jam, or waiting three-quarters of an hour for a bus – of all the things that infuriate people about living in a European city, among the highest-ranking must be congestion. The majority of people who work in cities spend at least an hour travelling to and from their jobs, and some more long-distance commuters spend over two hours every day in transit. But although individual journey times may be longer than we would like, the extraordinary ability of European urban transport systems to support the ceaseless daily expansion and contraction of the city's population borders on the fantastic.

The sheer volume of the city's elastic population is difficult to comprehend. In London each weekday morning, in the three hour period between 07.00 and 10.00, the number of people in the central area of the city swells by 1.3 million. The majority of these people are carried on public transport: 41% arrive on trains, 35% use the Underground, and 8% travel by bus; only 13% drive private cars, and 2% ride bicycles. It's possible to imagine, then, that commuter flow in London is hidden away below street level. But think about those figures another way: even if cyclists represent just one fiftieth of London's 1.3 million morning arrivals, they nonetheless amount to around 26,000 additional bicycles moving around the city centre during this part of the morning. Similarly, although the proportion of people using private cars makes up just 13% of commuters, this amounts to 130,000 additional cars in the city centre by 10.00.

And this movement of people around London doesn't stop at 10.00. The 'rush hour' is only the beginning of a steady increase in communal activity that peaks in the mid-afternoon, much of it involving short journeys which ensure pressure on the city's transport network is fairly constant. The cumulative statistics are breathtaking: during an average day, from 12,000 bus stops around the city, travellers make four million journeys on 5,000 buses; while below street level, with its 274 stations, 392km of track, 500 trains and a staff of 16,000, London Underground facilitates some 2.5 million journeys.

If this accumulation of statistical data begins to fade to a blur, it's worth remembering that all this movement, as well as being an essential factor in the way the cities are planned for the future, is equally one of the key reasons why our cities have developed their unique history. London looks like it does, and is organised in the way that it is, precisely because people have always moved around it. It may be the landmark buildings which characterise individual cities in our minds, but while Big Ben and Nelson's Column let us know we are in London, the way we move around these immobile monuments has been equally important in the definition of the city. London is London because of flux.

Still more people descend out of the sky onto London every day. The airports of Heathrow, Gatwick, Stansted, City and Luton welcome between them more than 100 million passengers a year. All these people, arriving in something calling itself 'London', have nevertheless – if they actually want to be in London – to make their way into the centre of the city. Ironically, almost the only places in London which announce you are actually in London are the airports – and most of them fall outside the administrative boundaries of the city. Heathrow and Gatwick are 80km apart, while Stansted is 85km from Heathrow by the shortest route. And the identity and location of 'Central London' shifts according to who is looking for it: a banker arriving in City airport due urgently at a meeting at Lloyds is almost there; a student arriving in Heathrow looking to learn English has a long trek up the Piccadilly Line to Leicester Square; a tourist shuttled in from Stansted has to find a route out of Liverpool Street station before they can even begin to negotiate their way through the crowds and 'bright lights' of the West End.

Although all of these locations embody a different 'centre' of London, none of them declare themselves as such. And London has many other undeclared centres – maybe as many as it has residents. For every person living in the city, daily life can support the sense that the idea of 'London' can be defined by reference to more than one geographical sector. The patch of streets in which someone works every day, or the area in which they go out drinking are more central to what they recognise as London than the notional 'heart of the city' peddled by tourist brochures. And in addition to these everyday centres, each of us carries in our head a shifting picture of an ideal, assimilated London, an abstraction we sense only sporadically in normal life: through the rain-smeared window of a late-night bar, or driving over the Thames at dusk. But these personal versions of essential London are undiluted by the recognition that The Mall, Oxford Street and Soho are all parts of the 'centre', the area we collectively agree to call the most 'London-like' of our city.

The 100 million airborne arrivals who descend on London each year are equal to almost twice the population of Britain. Travel on this scale now makes it impossible to characterise cities as stable entities. They're no longer simply geographical locations but urban contexts adapting themselves to constant flux. As much as it is a collection of buildings, a city is a shifting set of conceptual possibilities, robust enough to expand and contract on demand without losing its essential identity. But, predominantly, cities still seem to be pushing outwards: even back in 1845, Friedrich Engels had trouble finding "the beginning of the end" of London, feeling that it might be difficult for him to walk out of the city. Today, we know we haven't a hope of doing so. When one of London's airports is in fact in Cambridgeshire, with kilometres of rolling countryside in between, the city has become more a territory for the imagination than one with a measurable physicality.

Euralille: The 500 mile city

Where then is the edge of a city? As far as you can see? As far as you can think? As far as its transport network will take you? In 1989 Rem Koolhaas' practice OMA was

AIRPORT FACTFILE

AF001

Airport: Schiphol Airport
Airport code: LHR
Country: Netherlands
Runways: 5
Terminals: 1

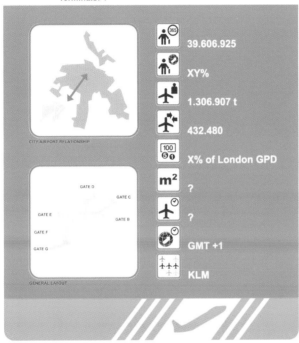

CITY-AIRPORT RELATIONSHIP

GATE D
GATE C
GATE E
GATE B
GATE F
GATE G

GENERAL LAYOUT

- 39.606.925
- XY%
- 1.306.907 t
- 432.480
- X% of London GPD
- ?
- ?
- GMT +1
- KLM

AIRLINE BAGGAGE IDENTIFICATION CHART

selected as the masterplanner for the redevelopment of
an enormous district in the French city of Lille.
Although the city's industrial-era staples of mining and
textiles had been in decline for decades, the project
coincided with the completion of the Channel Tunnel –
the resulting Eurostar train service would place Lille
at a strategically important nodal point in Europe's
transport network. At a stroke, this new city-within-a-
city – Euralille – found itself within 1.5 hours travel
time of over 50 million people located between London,
Brussels and Paris. Although Koolhaas' city was
developed in the middle of an existing one, it was to be
something entirely separate. Euralille's importance lies
not in where it is, but in where it leads to, and how long
it takes to get there. OMA's masterplan designated the
Eurostar railway station as an urban artery, placing a
set of high-profile buildings over the tracks, including
a vast shopping center, a congress hall and offices.

As an acknowledgement of the new city's status as a key
transport intersection, the trains weren't hidden in an
underground tunnel but celebrated with a transparent
station that wraps around a line cutting confidently
above ground – a bold design statement which reflected
Euralille's conceptual status as somewhere defined by
its relationship to international rather than local
structures. But Koolhaas' plan for this semi-detached
city has to coexist with more local needs. How does a
resident of Lille, one who spends 20 minutes walking to
work each day, engage with the fact that the new
'centre' of her city is actually closer timewise to
Brussels (18 minutes by train) than to her house down
the road? The metabolic rhythm of a city depends on its
sense of itself as a cohesive unit, as a community.
Cities usually accumulate around an abundance of raw
materials or the ability to trade services and skills,
but their survival depends on renewing these facilities

over time through continual (but often subconscious)
negotiation by its residents.

In the case of Lille, a city which grew up around the
abundance of natural resources which could be mined and
sold, this process of renewal has resulted in its
reinvention as a nodal point in European travel. But a
common agreement among Lille's population that the city
can thrive in this role has yet to materialise.
Euralille, for the moment more a giant version of a
motorway service station than a genuine city, should
eventually accrue a sense of community. Currently
though, it's sharply divided between the people who live
there, and the endless flow of outsiders the locals
observe simply passing through.

Cities demand that we move through them — arrival is
only the beginning — but great cities also make us stop.
It's possible to think of the urban tangle of early
morning commuting and the crowd of camera-clad visitors
outside Buckingham Palace as part of the same
affirmation of vitality. London's congestion increases
when its economy is booming, when the reasons for going
there are all the more compelling. And big cities are
always seductive. The tourist who gets their portrait
drawn in Leicester Square is not merely buying a picture
to take home, but the memento of an engagement with a
place that is powerfully semi-detached from reality.
This is not the London they have experienced in the form
of a grimy tube platform or an over-priced meal, but a
city built on expectations of glamour and excitement
they brought with them on the plane. As much as the stop
and start of buses and the arrival of commuter trains,
it is the unceasing daily accumulation of these kind of
encounters between people, the city and each other,
superimposed on the same static grid of streets, that
gives the city a sense of fluidity, of being 'alive'.

cinetrain
laurie
hawkinson

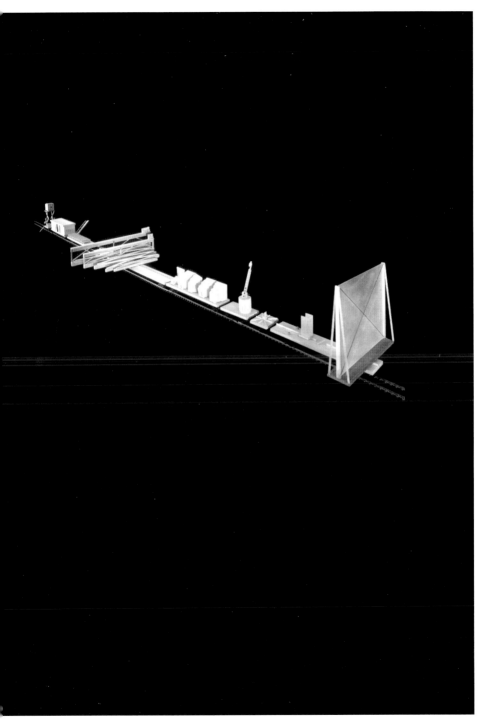

Las Meninas and the Cinematic Apparatus

The *Cinetrain* project began with the analysis of the painting *Las Meninas* by Velasquez of 1656, infamous for the inclusion of the painter and his canvas, disrupting the traditions of portraiture, and here relevant for its relationship to cinema. Leon Battista Alberti postulates that, "Painting is nothing but the intersection of the visual pyramid following a given distance, a fixed centre, and a certain lighting."[1] Velasquez short circuited Alberti's definition of painting by creating a paradox which involved the location of the fixed centre, either within or without of the painting field. In addition he asks, "Which direction is the visual pyramid projecting?"[2] This same question in the cinema, known as the shot-reverse shot asks, "Who is watching this, and who is ordering (editing) this?" Thus Velasquez's paradox anticipates cinema. Comparing a diagram of the painting in plan with a diagram of the viewer in relation to a screen (cinema), a multiplicity of readings for the identification of subjects and objects within and outside the painting is revealed. Sight lines (the visual pyramid) project from a subject represented as a mirror in the centre of the painting, implying it is the spectator who is 'outside'. Velasquez also uses the "double stage", where, "On one stage, the show is enacted, on the other the spectator looks at it."[3] However, in Velasquez's show, the painter (director) is included with the other characters and all are represented in the reverse-shot; a reaffirmation of the position of the subject. Thus the 'reality' of the painting is not what is represented, but rather a condition similar to that of a mirror/screen. In this reading the relationship of the viewer to the painting is that of the spectator to the screen, with the mirror in the painting imitating the condition of the moving beam emitting from the back of the movie theatre.

←←The cinematic apparatus is comprised of eight parts for the production and projection of film. The Cinetrain conforms to the travelling dimensions of the railroad; cars are ten feet wide and all parts fold to be less than 14 feet in height.

→The Camera Car (the subject). The camera can rotate and fix itself 360 degrees in any direction. The camera chair moves forward and back on the gantry arm. The space under the gantry is for the temporary storage of films.

1 Alberti, Leon Battista, *On Painting and on sculpture* (1435), Grayson, Cecil, ed and trans, London: Phaidon, 1972.

2 Alberti, *On Painting*.

3 Oudart, Jean-Pierre 1970.

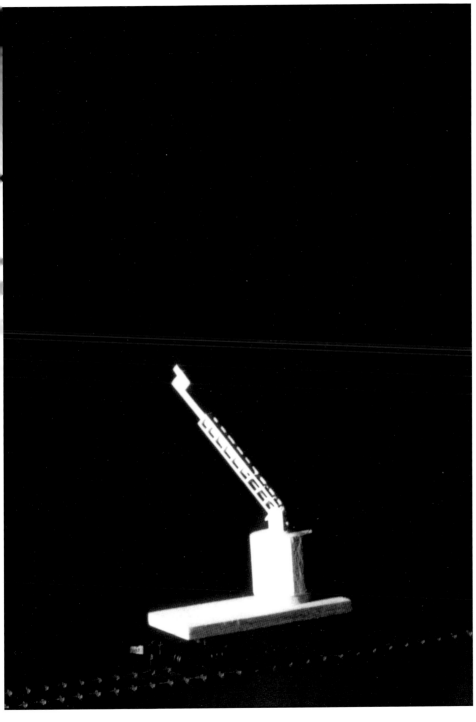

ROAM/G3.193

We, the spectators, are caught between the projector and
the screen. Stepping in front of the painting, we become
the subjects of the painting.

Cinetrain

If painting and sculpture were the medium of the
Renaissance, then surely film is the twentieth
century's biographer. Once film became a fact; that once
it altered our sense of time, space, narrative or anti-
narrative, it affected our way of seeing. The *Cinetrain*
project is an investigation into the relationship
between film and architecture.

The *Cinetrain* relates to the apparatus of cinema in its
eight cars specifically 'programmed' for the
production, projection and observation of film. The
Cinetrain conforms to the travelling dimensions of the
railroad; cars are ten feet wide and all parts fold to be
less than 14 feet in height. The cars are chosen from
existing railroad car types: the projector car, camera
car, and chair car from the work car; seating car from
the long bed flatcar; and the screen car from the
standardised flatbed car.

The tracks of the railroad are the site for the
Cinetrain. The *Cinetrain* carries film to a chosen
site and unfolds for use. The participants board the
train to view the film. The *Cinetrain* is also a machine
for making film and an educational tool for learning
about the filmmaking process. The eight parts combine
various ways for filming, editing and viewing. The
Cinetrain may operate perpendicular to the track so
that the cars operate in a 'field'. In this
configuration the cinematic apparatus simultaneously
films, edits and projects resulting in a process through
which the spectator becomes subject and object, both
actor and audience.

→The Projector Car can project up to three
film/images simultaneously. The car is able
to rotate 360 degrees and can fix itself
in any position, as well as move vertically
from zero to ten feet in elevation.

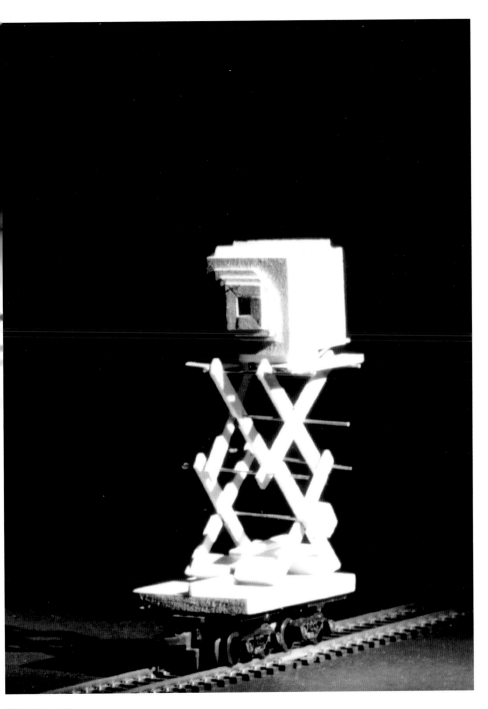

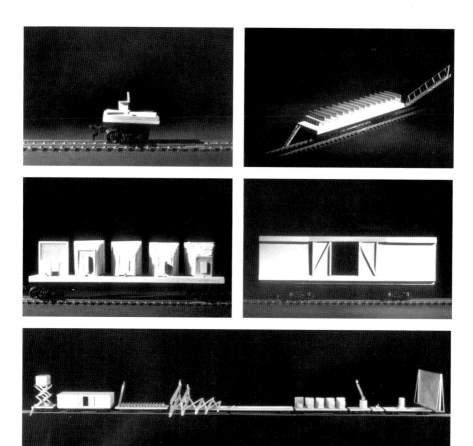

↑↑The Chair Car (the object) for the cameraman moves radially 360 degrees but can be fixed at 45 degree positions only. The chair can also slide forward and back on the radial tracks.

↑The Editing Car contains five rooms for editing film. Work being done in the editing car is visible through the screen from the outside. Screen, chair and editing table are movable on the track running the width of the car.

↑↑↑The Seating Car (the subject). Seating rotates 360 degrees but as the screen can only be fixed at positions perpendicular or parallel to the track.

↑↑The Equipment Car is a standard boxcar for bringing lights, props, film, or any other film apparatus to the film/cinema site.

↑Eight cars for the production and projection of film.

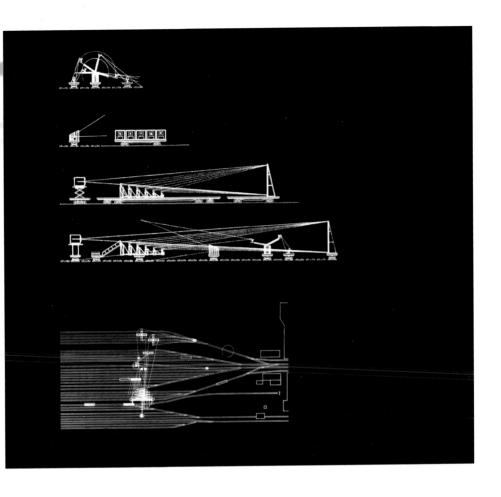

Project in plan demonstrating an in-line car configuration where film is projected along the railway track. Such a configuration is typical of an en-route, that is between stations.

Plan demonstrating parallel car configuration where film is projected perpendicular to the railway track. Such a configuration is typical of the spatial organisation of a goods yard or that around a station and its platforms.

transferium
falk
schneeman

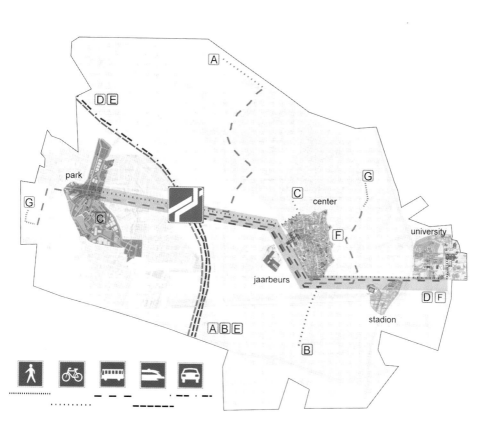

Ⓐ home - maglev
1.7 km bike   6 min
4.5 km bus   10 min
1 km bus conv   1 min
7.2 km = 17min + 1 staps

Ⓑ home - maglev
1.7 km bike   6 min
4 km bus conv   4 min
5.7 km = 10min + 1 stap

Ⓒ home - park
6.5 km bike   20 min
6.5 km = 20min

Ⓓ university - maglev
0.5 km walking   8 min
9 km bus conv   9 min
9.5 km = 17min + 1 staps

Ⓔ A2 - maglev
1 stap 5 -10 min

Ⓕ home - university
4.5 km bike   14 min
4.5 km = 14 min

Ⓖ home - friend
0.75 km bike   6 min
5 km bus   12 min
8 km bus conv   8 min
13.75 km = 26min + 1 stap

modal conveyor
a toolbox

climb

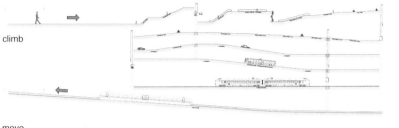

move

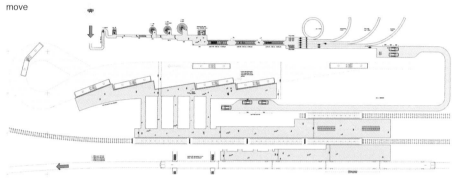

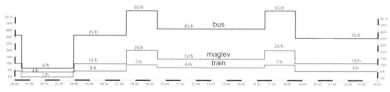

timetable

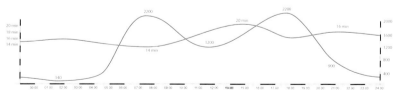

number of people and average duration of stay

The Dutch cities of Amsterdam, Den Haag, Rotterdam and Utrecht form the compact 'metroloop' popularly referred to as the Randstad, or 'Rim City', Europe's densest conurbation. A number of government initiatives have investigated the potential for a high speed magnetic levitation ('maglev') rail system to solve the growing mobility problem in this rapidly expanding urban cluster. The *Transferium* is a design proposal by Falk Schneemann for an interchange in Utrecht, located at the intersection of maglev, railway, highway and local traffic networks. The *Transferium* is sited on the border between the historic city, with 350,000 inhabitants, and a new quarter, with 75,000 inhabitants. Although the *Transferium* is designed for a specific site it can also be seen as an urban prototype, configurable to other locations and transfer modes.

In the *Transferium,* excessive consumption of valuable realty is avoided by the spatial economics of the station's vertical organisation. This results in a footprint 50% smaller than that of a traditional station with a similar number of platforms. To avoid the congestion typical around a railway station, the *Transferium* creates an 'urban conveyor', with the four transfer modes – maglev train, train, bus and car – over four stacked levels.

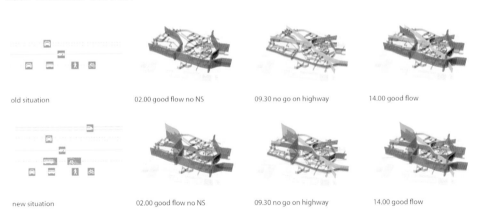

old situation   02.00 good flow no NS   09.30 no go on highway   14.00 good flow

new situation   02.00 good flow no NS   09.30 no go on highway   14.00 good flow

mobile sketch pad
dominic trevett

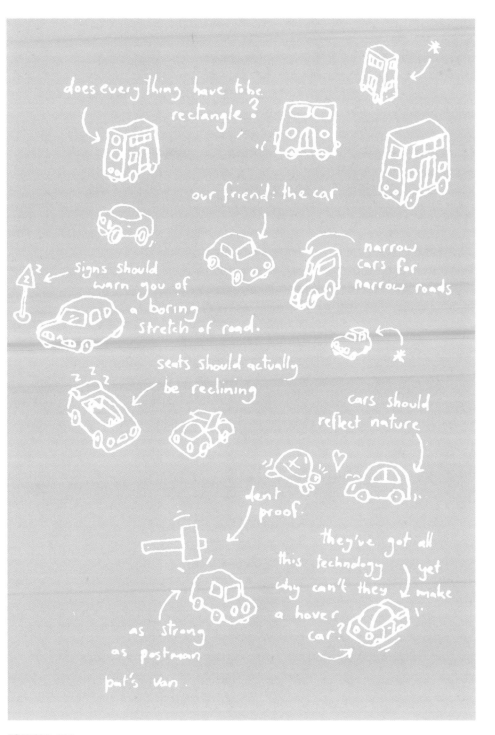

true wings

giant cover to keep plane nice and warm.

dad's sock

wind driven → sail

blend in with the natural world. as standard.

all planes would be fitted with stuff.

Aesthistically pleasing

the flying dough nut

duel-end plane - so no need to turn around.

big windows so you can see

destination moon

dries your clothes as well

onboard kebab

room for your pets.

for safaris 4x4 bus

solid wings

relax man onboard café.

mini-bus: weaves in and out of traffic.

many more safety features

seats 700

comfy seats

jumbo bus

decent suspension

balcony: need a breath of fresh air.

helibus pad

bionic bus

the bus should be a portable office

school theme bus

helibus

inspiration should be taken from classics

round off all edges

takes you anywhere.

the big bus

does everything have to be rectangle?

faster service

our friend: the car

forget metallic

bright lights that don't dazzel

signs should warn you of a boring stretch of road.

narrow cars for narrow roads

no more flats

self inflating

seats should actually be reclining

cars should reflect nature

a car with a perfect radio

a sports car that seats more than one person

one way of solving conjestion

dent proof.

they've got all this technology yet why can't they make a hover car?

tall roofs are needed

as strong as postman pat's van.

rain powered imagine how far you'll get

GATE
FOUR

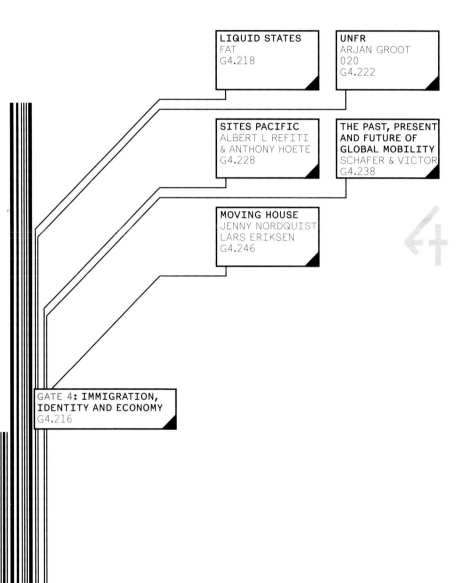

LIQUID STATES
FAT
G4.218

UNFR
ARJAN GROOT
020
G4.222

SITES PACIFIC
ALBERT L REFITI
& ANTHONY HOETE
G4.228

THE PAST, PRESENT
AND FUTURE OF
GLOBAL MOBILITY
SCHAFER & VICTOR
G4.238

MOVING HOUSE
JENNY NORDQUIST
LARS ERIKSEN
G4.246

GATE 4: IMMIGRATION,
IDENTITY AND ECONOMY
G4.216

immigration

identity

and economy

Against a backdrop of motion, the question of identity as mediated through place is visited. So how mobile, exactly, is the contemporary world? If mobility is quantified in terms of a 'passenger odometer', then the average annual distance travelled by each of earth's inhabitants was, in 1950, 1,334 passenger kilometres. This is equivalent to a daily commute of 3.6 kilometres per person. Today, the mobility of the world's population has surpassed 4,781 kilometres per year, or over 13 kilometres per person per day.[1]

What drives this demand for mobility in the twenty-first century? The rapid growth of the world's population, from 2.52 billion 50 years ago to 6.06 billion today, and the steady migration towards cities has meant increased urbanisation: in 2000, 46% of the planet was urbanised; with 75% of inhabitants in the industrialised world living in urban areas.[2]

Within this context, the idea of identity originating from place is being challenged. The borders of regional zones are no longer seen through the framework of local versus global but are semantic poles of a continuum in which geo-political and spatio-economic flows are occurring.[3] With this in mind, a "Universal authority for National Flag Registration" has been established by Arjan Groot of O2O to meet the future accelerated demand for international reformations. States are either undermined or underlined by these geo-political and spatio-economic flows, as illustrated by FAT's *Liquid States*. Similarly, the spatial identity of "Sites Pacific®", formulated through the electronic missives between Albert Refiti and WHAT Architecture, is founded upon the borderlessness of oceanic, rather than land-based, exchange: "to be located in and around the Pacific is to confront the undifferentiated abyss that is the ocean". The ocean is the ground in Polynesia and has the ability to "rise up to decompose the face of identity".[4]

2 UN Populations Division.

3 www.yale.edu/ycias/cbi/unbound.htm.

4 Deleuze, Giles, Difference and Repetition, Paul Patton, trans, New York: Columbia University Press, 1968/1994.

In 20 years time, the global passenger odometer will have more than doubled at 10,500 passenger kilometres per person per year! Travel will increasingly be determined by the principle of an urban transportation model pioneered by Yacov Zahavi. This model proposes the idea of mobility as 'temporal economics' – the idea that fixed budgets of time and money are devoted to travel. This is examined in *The Past and Future of Global Mobility* by the research scientists Andreas Schafer and David G Victor who have been comparing the levels of mobility across the world's geographic territories: travel distances, relative wealth and dominant modalities.

liquid
states
fat

The animation of the world's continents
as one geographic territory
constitutes FAT's Liquid States.
Originally formatted as an interactive
web piece, ROAM re-presents this shape
shifting map as a sequence of
timeframes. Existing coastlines are
morphologically reorganised such that
borders dissolve into a collage of
equally familiar and unknown states.
The contribution relies upon the iconic
status of maps, and their formal
blankness – a 'mute' aesthetic – in
relation to their geographic, political
and social associations. Morphing
between these episodic fragments
recalls timescales both of plate
tectonics and instantaneous electronic
communications. This map suggests
landscapes as fluid as capital, as
connected as cell phone networks.
A map of collapsing geography.

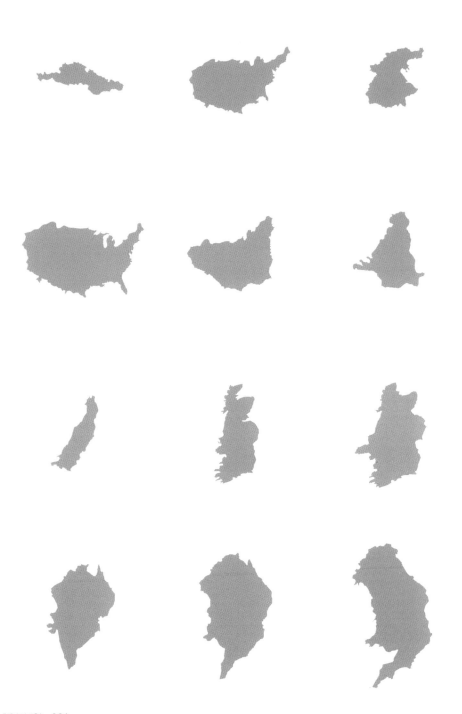

unfr
arjan groot
020

UNFR: Universal Authority for Flag Registration

CODING SYSTEM

Each flag in the UNFR is connected to a code that consists of eleven characters. This is how the code is composed.

→ The first character of the UNFR code is always a letter that stands for the background colour of the flag.

→ The second, third and fourth characters are a letter and two numbers, that indicate colour and shape of the pattern that is on top of the background colour. If there is no pattern on the flag, there are three zeros.

→ Next, the code contains two times three characters, which are composed in the same way as described in the previous paragraph. This part of the code indicates optional patterns that cover the first pattern. If the flag doesn't have extra patterns, these characters are zeros.

→ The last character is a letter that indicates the colour of the symbol on the flag. If there's no symbol, then this character is also a zero.

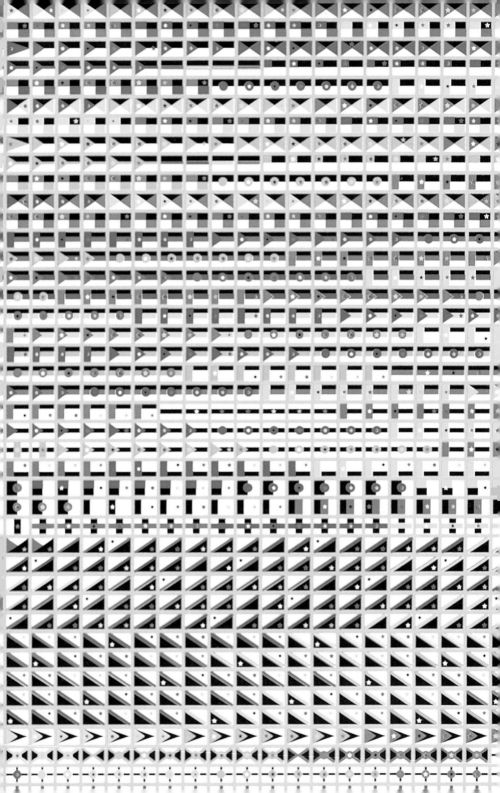

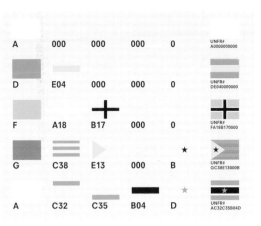

A	000	000	000	0	UNFR# A0000000000
D	E04	000	000	0	UNFR# DE040000000
F	A18	B17	000	0	UNFR# FA18B170000
G	C38	E13	000	B	UNFR# GC38E13000B
A	C32	C35	B04	D	UNFR# AC32C35B04D

Index System

The standarised flags in the UNFR index are composed of seven basic colours and forty basic patterns. With the selection of these colours and patterns, the designs of existing national flags in the year 2000 have been taken into account.

A flag in the UNFR index is composed as follows:

→   a background pattern.
→   a pattern in any of the other 6 colours, or a combination of patterns, with a maximum of 3.
→   a symbol (optional) in one colour.

In this system, symbols are designated by five pointed stars. These stars can represent any possible symbol (or group of symbols, e.g., a cluster of stars, or a moon and a star), providing that it has only one colour. The shape of the symbol and its place on the flag are not relevant for the position of the flag in the index. Only the symbol's colour determines this.

Theoretically, this system produces many thousands of millions of combinations, the majority of which are not suitable to serve as flags, from an aesthetic point of view. UNFR has catalogued 177,489 acceptable flags. Of those, 172 have been reserved for UN member countries.

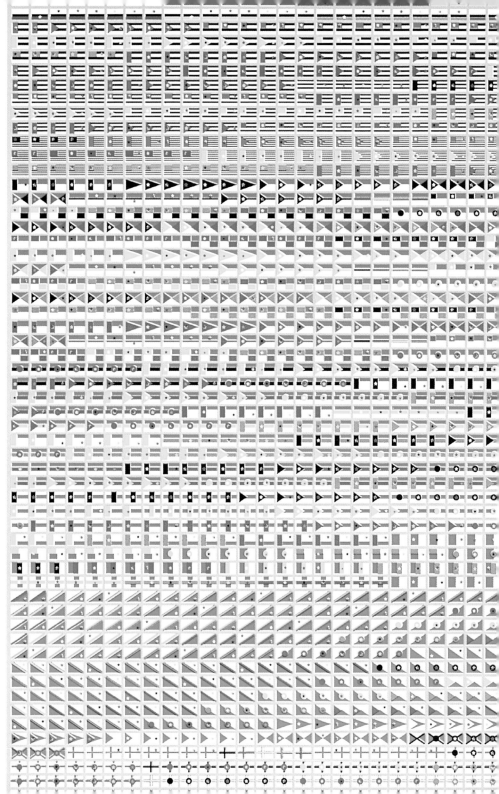

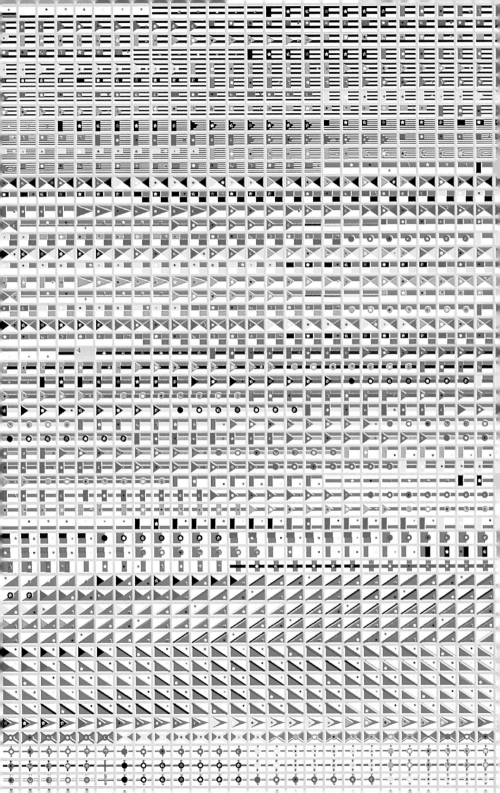

sites
pacific
albert l
refiti and
anthony
hoete

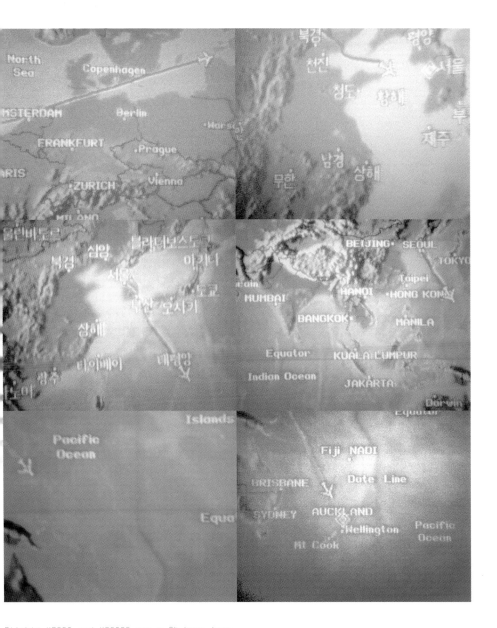

Flights KE908 and KE8823 are a 24-hour long
haul flight from London Heathrow to
Auckland, New Zealand via Seoul, Korea.

Sites Pacific® refers to the formalisation of a specific South Pacific spatial identity. A transitional space, a space in motion, 'beach-like', lacking clearly demarcated borders or edges. A space of ebb and flow, an identity borne out of a tide of cultural insecurity and spatial schizophrenia triggered by the idea of distance. This 'long-haul' text attempts to relocate the reader to this 'other world' within the largest geographic feature on earth.[1] Sites Pacific® are as far as you are likely to travel – commonly signposted 'the Antipodes' as if it were a location, a site, rather than a place, that by definition, ought to be at the other side of the world.[2]

1 The Pacific Ocean covers nearly one third of the world's surface area and is larger than the total of all its land areas.

2 ROAM distribution demographic says that you are likely to be reading this footnote predominantly in the EU or the US.

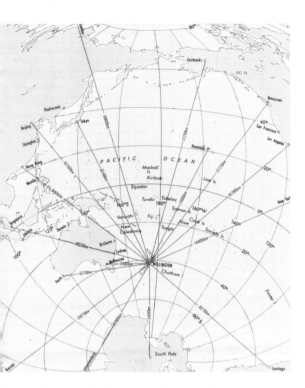

Condition 1: Sites Pacific® refers to an oceanic rather than a land-based spatial identity.

Political space as exercised in Europe, Asia and the Americas coincides with bounded land territories; in the South Pacific, the notion of nation arises out of cultural and social exchanges founded upon the instabilities and borderlessness of an oceanic existence. Political space exercised in the South Pacific is demarcated in fishing rights, exclusive economic zones and military waters. Thus oceanic territories are as numerous as those which are land-based.

Great Circle Distances from Aukland.
Great Circle distances underline the
relative isolation of Sites Pacific as
small places, a long way away: London 18810
kilometres, New York 14,400 kilometres,
Melbourne 2,580 kilometres.

To be located in and around the Pacific is to confront the undifferentiated abyss that is the ocean. Of all grounds it is the most insubstantial because it has no fixed identity, no stable position(s), and as Mike Austin suggested "boundaries are not easily drawn on its surface".[2] If anything the sea serves and severs the will to identity and tends to multiply and confuse the specificity of location – the oceanscape always pushes you hither and thither and one literally floats on it. Polynesians designate the ocean as the va or wa; an opening, a gap or in-between place that dislocates and disconnects people and things, not in a negative way but as a reality that provides a way to bond them 'positively'. In the Samoa Islands the ocean is vasa – translated as sacred gap: va – gap, sa – sacred.[3] Canoes and voyaging crafts are known as va'a or waka, things that bridge this in-between space. The ocean is the ground in Polynesia, not the grounding of stability but the "undifferentiated abyss" that Deleuze say has the ability to "rise up to decompose the face of identity".[4]

Polynesian mythological map.

2 Austin, M R, Polynesian Architecture in New Zealand, doctoral thesis, New Zealand: University of Auckland, 1976.

3 Wendt, A, "Tatauing the Post-Colonial Body", unpublished paper from the Bodies in Question Conference, Department of Art History, University of Auckland, 1996.

4 Deleuze, G, Difference and Repetition, Paul Patton trans, New York: Columbia University Press, 1968/1994.

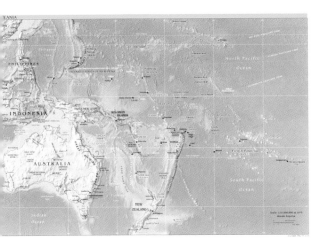

Condition 2: Sites Pacific® are defined by points, or islands, rather than lines, or borders.

5 see Paul Virilio, "The Overexposed City", below.

Islands, or *motu*, which literally translates as "to sever" or "break" as well as "to stand on" or "to erect on", are the product of identification. Fished out of the sea (Maori) and thrown from heaven (Samoa) it is where land or *whenua* is fought over and contested. So if the sea is the designated ground of Polynesia, then island is form, the determined object of placement and identity.

A South Pacific island is couched in a certain romanticism, from Robert Louis Stevenson's domestication of Treasure Island through to the escapism of the desert island, a lyrical site offering refuge and relief. What is mobility then in this quaint Polynesian schema? Well, mobility here is not so concerned with the "aesthetic of disappearance", or the fixed relation of a body with 'movement-space' but with a conceptualisation of the world and objects revolving around the navigator at sea.[5] Mobility conceptualised in this fashion suggests that the navigator's subject-position is one of fixity in the

Sites Pacific® are characterised by an architecture of the archipelago, of oceanic rather than land-based cultural exchange.

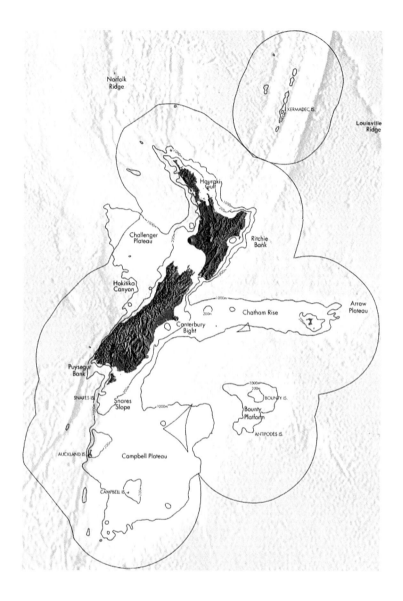

Norfolk
Ridge

Louisville
Ridge

KERMADEC IS.

Hauraki
Gulf

Challenger
Plateau

Ritchie
Bank

Hokitika
Canyon

Arrow
Plateau

Chatham Rise

Canterbury
Bight

Puysegur
Bank

SNARES IS

Snares
Slope

BOUNTY IS.

Bounty
Platform

ANTIPODES IS.

AUCKLAND IS.

Campbell Plateau

CAMPBELL IS.

The sea demarcated as an Exclusive
Economic Zone provides a graphic depiction
of maritime jurisdiction. For relatively
small South Pacific island states, the
projection of the coastline 200 kilometres
out to sea provides a crucial extension of
economic resources.

moment event. He fixes himself to the flux of nature and
the world of motion is made to revolve around the eye of
experience, and time and space is extracted from the
rising mass beneath him.[6]

6 www.sacred-texts.
com/pac/grey/grey
04.htm. The rising
mass alludes to the
demigod Maui, who
according to legend
loved to fish. One
day his fishing line
caught, and when he
pulled, each of the
Hawaiian Islands
broke the surface of
the sea.

Condition 3: In order to ensure survival, island networks arise to form an architecture of the archipelago.

The night sky of the South Pacific is rendered black by
the lack of ambient light, punctuated by intensely
bright stars. These celestial constellations reflected
in the ocean's surface seemingly map the large
groupings of sparsely populated, island worlds. The
space of this archipelago is defined by some 4000
islands including American Samoa, Cook Islands, Fiji
Islands, Kiribati, New Caledonia, Niue, Papua New Guinea,
Samoa, Solomon Islands, Tahiti, Tonga, Tuvalu, Vanuatu
and Aotearoa. This network of small island worlds,
positioned through the sky and located in the sea, mean
that the concept of 'nation' resides within
na(viga)tion.

Ships which once used the islands as oceanic stop-overs,
'maiden' voyages and re-fuelling points no longer do so
as advances in marine technologies render such places
'ghost islands' and parallel the highway's bypassing of
the small town. To counter eternal remoteness, Sites
Pacific® have sporned an insatiable desire for
information, unreservedly absorbing new forms of
communication as a means of bridging distance via
remote control and re-establishing a sense of identity.
The fishing net has been forsaken for that of the
internet recasting what was once 'island' — ex-*ile* — as
'mainland'.

Condition 4: The dominant means to bridge and connect the archipelago network is via the metaphor.
As a counterpoint to western epistemology and its theories of knowledge, Sites Pacific® are open to interpretative modes. Speculative and slippery, a metaphor – from the Greek *metaphorae* meaning to carry – produces transferable conditions that are utopian, ideal and paradisiacal. Except here the metaphor is less a bridge than a boat travelling in an oratory current of traditional storytelling and myth making. The stories didn't travel so far and thus formed localised identities, transcribed as *tattoo*. The tattoo was an encoded message, the wearer at best a carrier, at worst a passenger. Together it was a mode, a transportable communications device. A message without the use of text.

Tattooing in the Pacific is a communal act, the body is inscribed with a communal code and made to open up to the community – a tattooed body is a transparent thing. The tattoo in Polynesia is not about the consolidation of the individual (as in contemporary manifestations of tattooing) but the opening up of the individual to the community, your soul resides on the surface for everyone to see and not hidden on the inside. Here, to communicate demanded an engagement with the communal, a public space. The tattooed body is a dazzling object that confuses the stable reading of the real body from its pattern; the inscribed skin in movement confuses the surface from the object. The person is literally made to be mobile, displaced from himself, given time and made to float in the sea of collective signifiers.

This is not dislocation as if something is severed from its source – the islander like the navigator is already suspended on the instability of the sea, with the politics of location and identity already having displaced 'place'. This is dislocation as a condition of repetition, as a continual return to a type of seasickness, to be giddy with motion. The Pacific navigator like the tattooed person acquires mobility by stasis, by virtue of his immobility. The mobile is consumed into him in the form of mass and space and in the form of time (lines).

Condition 5: Sites Pacific® pollinate the idea of a brave new world.

Characterised by the founding imprint of indigenous peoples and interwoven with the transformations arising from settlement by peoples from elsewhere, Auckland functions as the migratory hub for Sites Pacific®. There are more Cook Islanders, Niueans and Tokelauans in Auckland than 'back home', and so this sprawling conglomeration is declared its capital.[7] Auckland is officially the largest Polynesian city in the world and thus is a city where 'the Polynesian' is the emerging cultural identity, debunking a colonial heritage, to become the spatial unifier for a new form of 'polynation'. Auckland has one of the highest ratios of city versus national population in the world thanks to Pacific migration and urbanisation that have prompted 28% of the population to amass in one city centre. Not exactly a country nor a complicit member state, this a territory of geo-political overlap – a Venn diagram form of intersectional space – whereby a strategic location accumulates and urbanises to become the principal node servicing multiple nations and multiple identities. The green and blue image of New Zealand, of beaches and bush, upheld by the local tourist board contradicts the fact that the country is more urbanised (85%) than Europe (74%) or Japan (78%) leaving the rural identity well and truly outdated.[8] Sites Pacific® is transformational space operating at a scale beyond national identity.

7 A distinction is hereby made: Wellington is the capital of New Zealand whilst Auckland is the proposed capital of Sites Pacific®.

8 United Nations Populations Division 1997.

the past and future of global mobility andreas schafer and david victor

How much will people travel in the future? Which modes of transport will they use? Where will traffic be most intense? The answers are critical for planning infrastructures and for assessing the consequences of mobility. They will help societies anticipate environmental problems, such as acid rain and global warming, which are partially caused by transport emissions. These questions also lie at the centre of efforts to estimate the future size of markets for transportation hardware: aircraft, automobiles, buses and trains.

In our research, we have tried to answer these questions for 11 geographic regions specifically and, more generally, for the world. One of us (Schafer) compiled historical statistics for all four of the principal motorised modes of transportation – trains, buses, automobiles and high-speed transport (aircraft and high-speed trains, which we place in a single category because both could eventually offer mobility at comparable quality and speed). Together we used this unique database to compose a scenario for the future volume of passenger travel, as well as the relative prevalence of different forms of transportation through the year 2050. Our perspective was both long term and large scale because transport infrastructures evolve slowly, and the effects of mobility are increasingly global. The answers to those fundamental questions, we found, largely depend on only a few factors.

Historical data suggests that, throughout the world, personal income and traffic volume grow in tandem. As average income increases, the annual distance travelled per capita by car, bus, train or aircraft (termed motorised mobility, or traffic volume) rises by roughly the same proportion. The average North American earned US $9,600 and travelled 12,000km (7,460 miles) in 1960; by 1990 both per capita income and traffic volume had approximately doubled.

In developing countries the relation has been less tight. Between 1960 and 1990 the average income in China tripled, but motorised traffic volume rose ten-fold, to 630km. This discrepancy reflects, in part, the fact that growing wealth allows the poor to substitute motorised mobility, typically by bus or train, for non-motorised forms such as walking and biking, for which the statistics are notoriously unreliable and, so, are excluded from our database.

The charted relation between income and traffic volume affirms a postulate by the late analyst Yacov Zahavi: on average, humans devote a roughly predictable fraction of their expenditures to transportation. This fraction is typically three to five percent in developing countries, where people rely predominantly on non-motorised and public transportation. The fraction rises with automobile ownership, stabilising at 10 to 15% at ownership levels of 0.2 car per capita (one car per family of five). Nearly all members of the Organisation for Economic Cooperation and Development (OECD), the rich industrial nations, have completed this automobile transition. Figures from the US, for example, show that this fraction remained nearly constant even during the two oil-price shocks of the 1970s; travellers compensated for higher operating costs by demanding less expensive (and more fuel-efficient) vehicles.

This predictable relation between income and transport spending allowed us to conjecture plausibly about the future. In the absence of major economic upsets, traffic volume should continue to rise with income, as in the past. Using reasonable assumptions for future income growth, we estimated that traffic volume in North America will rise to 58,000 passenger kilometres a year in 2050. In China, annual motorised mobility will reach 4,000 passenger-kilometres, which is comparable with Western European levels in the mid 1960s. Developing countries will contribute a rising share to global traffic volume because, although their per capita mobility will remain lower, both their populations and their average incomes will grow faster than those of OECD nations. In 1960 the developing countries could claim only 22% of the world traffic volume, but by 2050, we estimate, they will account for about half of it.

Higher Incomes, Higher Speeds

How will people satisfy the growing demand for mobility? We searched for patterns in how modes of transportation compete. Again, Zahavi offered a useful starting point: he argued that people devote on average a constant fraction of their daily time to travel, what he called the travel-time budget. All the reliable surveys that we have found support this hypothesis: the travel-time budget is typically between 1.0 and 1.5 hours per person per day in a wide variety of economic, social and geographic settings. Residents of African villages have a travel-time budget similar to those of Japan, Singapore, Western Europe and North America. Small groups and individuals vary in their behaviour, but at the level of aggregated populations, a person spends an average of 1.1 hours a day travelling.

If people hold their time for travel constant but also demand more mobility as their income rises, they must select faster modes of transport to cover more distance in the same time. At low incomes (below $5,000 per capita), motorised travel is dominated by buses and low-speed trains that, on average, move station-to-station at approximately 20 to 30kph. As income rises, slower public transport modes are replaced by automobiles, which typically operate door-to-door at 30 to 55kph and offer greater flexibility. (These average speeds, which vary by region, are lower than the posted speed limits because of congestion and other inefficiencies.) The share of traffic volume supplied by automobiles peaks at approximately $10,000 per capita. At higher incomes, aircraft and high-speed trains supplant slower modes.

At present, aircraft supply 96% of all high-speed transport, flying airport-to-airport at about 600kph. Although the constancy of the travel-time budget pushes people with rising incomes toward faster modes of transportation, the share of motorised mobility that each mode holds is strongly determined by geography. In the late 1950s, when Jack Kerouac extolled the open road in America, relatively few kilometres were motored by other means: by the 1960s, private automobiles delivered 90% of North American traffic volume because the continent had plenty of space and plenty of roads. In contrast, in more densely populated Western Europe, the share of automobiles never climbed so high: it has been stagnant at about 70% and is poised to decline. Asia is even more compact, with an urban density three times that of Western Europe. Accordingly, we expect that automobiles will peak at only 55% of the total traffic volume in the high-income Pacific OEGD nations, which is primarily attributable to Japan. Public transport will continue to account for a higher share of mobility in Asia than in less densely populated regions.

In addition, the availability of roads, railways, airports and other essential infrastructures constrains the transport choices. Because transport infrastructures are expensive and long-lived, it typically takes six to seven decades to eliminate them (for example, canals) or to make new ones (for example, roads). New infrastructures could be built for a radically different transportation system by late in the twenty-first century, but transport choices for the next 20 to 30 years will be limited by earlier investments.

On the Move in 2050

Assuming that a constant travel-time budget, geographic constraints and short-term infrastructure constraints persist as fundamental features of global mobility, what long-term results can one expect? In high-income regions, notably North America, our scenario suggests that the share of traffic volume supplied by buses and automobiles will decline as high-speed transport rises sharply. In developing countries, we anticipate the strongest increase to be in the share first for buses and later for automobiles. Globally, these trends in bus and automobile transport are partially offsetting. From 1960 to 2050 the share of world traffic volume by buses will remain roughly constant, whereas the automobile share will decline only gradually to 35%. High-speed transport should account for about 40% of all passenger kilometres travelled in 2050. In all regions, the share of low-speed rail transport will probably continue its evident decline.

Despite the sharply rising share of air travel, other types of vehicles, including automobiles, will remain crucial parts of the transportation system. Even in North America, where we expect the relative decline of automobiles to be steepest, the absolute traffic volume supplied by cars will decline only after peaking at 22,000 passenger kilometres per person in 2010. By 2050, automobiles will still supply 14,000 passenger kilometres per person, which means that North Americans will be driving as much as they did in 1970.

The allocation of travel time reflects the continuing importance of low-speed transport. We expect that from 1990 through to 2050, the average North American will continue to devote most of his or her 1.1 hour travel time budget to automobile travel. The very large demand for air travel (or high-speed rail travel) that will be manifest in 2050 works out to only 12 minutes per person a day; a little time goes a long way in the air. In several developing regions, most travel time in 2050 will still be devoted to non-motorised modes. Buses will persist as the primary form of motorised transportation in developing countries for decades. No matter how important air travel becomes, buses, automobiles and even low-speed trains will surely go on serving vital niches. Some of the super-rich already commute and shop in aircraft, but most people will continue to spend most of their travel time on the ground.

moving house
jenny nordquist
lars eriksen

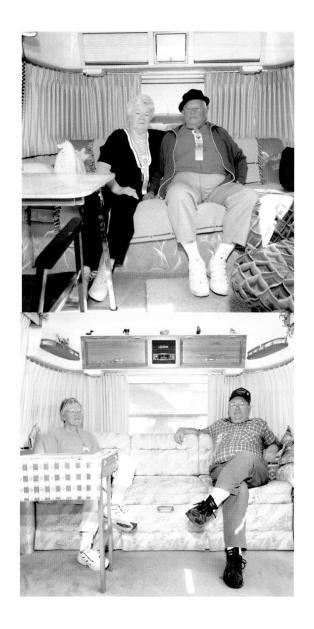

Once a year, a small desert town in the heart of
Arizona becomes the Mecca for a group of devoted
caravan owners. Quartzite, which boasts a population
of 2,300 during the off-peak season, becomes the home
to more than a million recreational vehicle
enthusiasts during the month of January when the
rocky soil and bareness of the gloomy desert softens
up in a visual feast. Just for a short while man
defies nature, and the glorious sight of fake palm
trees, the green, green grass of astro-turf and
adorable plastic ducks transcends what nature seemed
to have destined for an eternity of austerity. They
all gather here: the 'snowbirds' flying down from the
rigours of a Midwestern winter; the 'full-timers' who
have uprooted themselves from anything that could be
considered conventional real estate; and the
'Airstreamers' in glorious space age containers with
their shiny soft edges. As they all gather around
their spiritual Cabba, the caravan culture which they
have devoted their life to, time comes to a
standstill, and the world outside Quartzite, Arizona
loses its final traces of relevance.

There is something magical about silver Airstream
caravans. Their voluptuous appearance fits perfectly
into the awesome American scenery. The interaction
between vehicle, nature and fake garden ornaments
creates a dream-like simulation, a strange hyper-
reality where nature becomes artificial and artifice
becomes natural.

What drives these people to eschew the conventions
of home and household and take their American dream
out on the road? This was not a simple question of
isolation as escape from the traumas of middle class
existence or the daunting obligations of civil
society. The motivations for inhabiting the limited

space of a recreational vehicle appeared to relate
less to any thirst for seclusion and much more to
the pursuit of adventure in mystical hybrid that is
America, an adventure that was worth being shared in
a mobile community. In parallel with those that
Alexis De Tocqueville encountered on his journeys
into the vastness of nineteenth century America in
"A Fortnight in the Wilds", the 'caravaners' seek
the edges of this great nation in which to live out
their dream. America, the beautiful! America, the
desert! Only this strange landscape of vast
ambiguity does the caravan and its people true
justice. Only out here, at the outskirts of human
control, does the beauty of a sublime collaboration
between the infinity of the natural and the
artificial emerge. In his book, America, Jean
Baudrillard touches upon this notion of the desert
as an endless neutrality. "Why are the deserts so
fascinating? It is because you are delivered from
all depth there – a brilliant, mobile, superficial
neutrality, a challenge to meaning and profundity,
a challenge to nature and culture, an outer
hyperspace, with no origin, no reference-points."

Yet on the concrete of Las Vegas parking lots or in
the deserts of Arizona, the next generation of
caravan parks are arising in the American frontier,
offering caravan owners a more comfortable and
stylised alternative to the utopian notion of
nature's own camp ground. These 'new' environments
are built on a solid foundation of capitalistic
consumer culture. They provide all the necessary
complements to a happy holiday for the whole family:
swimming pools, fast-food restaurants and the odd
casino – twenty-four hours a day of unlimited
carelessness. Now the physical space of the caravan
becomes an identification of socio-economic relations

among the owners. While some manage to afford the
convenience of a modernised caravan park with
facilities galore or possess the financial resources
to invest in luxuriously equipped vehicles, still
others have to settle for more moderate means of
mobile housing and find themselves restricted to
limited areas of limited amenities. Even though both
breeds of caravaners meet in places like Quartzite,
share the same roads and the same nature, there
seems to exist a strange class-separation in caravan
society. Strange in the sense that caravan culture
appears to be founded on social values with a strong
sense of community, but not so strange when the
phenomenon is contextualised within the broader
perspective of American society.

The upholding of an idealised, harmonious home,
associated with specific values and social
relations, may create a perfect place of
identification for some, a prison for others.
Home is ever-changing in the world of the
recreational vehicle. The personalised caravan with
its tacky ornaments and plastic plants can resemble
a Catholic funeral parlour, decorated with glamour
and wonderful vanity, the perfect metaphor for a
fake reality. Alternatively, it can constitute a
pragmatic adaptation of the suburban picket-fence
bourgeois household inserted into the boldness of
the American landscape. The personalising of the
caravan provides the owner with the necessary
comforts of household, while simultaneously
maintaining mobility and accessibility to its
surroundings. Whichever type of space we choose to
inhabit, we have an essential need to represent our
culture and traditions through objects and
customisation. Since the caravan space is mass
produced there is even more incentive to introduce

unique distinctions from the standard form,
personalisations may revive past memories but may
also self-consciously project a certain appearance.
When massive Airstreams are being equipped with top
of the range kitchens and Jacuzzis, it is not done
in an effort to make life on the road more
comfortable. The fact is that the only places where
you can actually take full advantage of these
technological wonders are in the modern state-of-
the-art caravan parks, which have the necessary
hook-ups but which also offer the temptation of
hotel rooms at the same prices. If the authentic
dynamic of the caravan is in enabling a home to
move, in rendering nomadic what is typically
sedentary, then this tendency is an ironic insult to
the true spirit of the game.

The home on the road is a glorious home. It is a
home founded on ideals of liberation and expedition,
convenience and luxury, independence and community,
inertia and mobility. But it may also be a dying
phenomenon. When the Airstream caravan was
advertised in the 1950s it was presented as the
perfect holiday experience for young, active people.
Today it is hard to find any 'caravaners' under the
age of 60. Yet the dream lives on, and the awesome
silver box still strolls across the highways
bringing Americans together in pursuit of adventure
– a physical salute to the possibilities of moving
home. Exit here.

HOMES DIRECT
YOUR FAVOURITE HOME DELIVERY - FOR LESS!

PLEASE QUOTE:
THE FOLLOWING REFERENCE **HD - R.O.A.M** *03*

QUICK ORDER FORM

FREE CONSULTATION   CRUISES AND TOURS   TRAVELLERS AND GIFT CHEQUES   MEMBERSHIP REWARDS -> JOIN THE IAS

ORDERED BY:

ACCOUNT NR:
YOUR NAME:
LOCATION:
ZIP CODE:
COUNTRY:

Tick here if address has changed from last order

Tick here if catalogues should be posted to this address

DELIVER TO: If different from ordered by

ACCOUNT NR:
YOUR NAME:
LOCATION:
ZIP CODE:
COUNTRY:

Tick here if catalogues should be posted to this address

E - MAIL:

PURCHA
ORDER N

ORDER
DATE.:

COST
CODEs.:

GET MOVING. YOU'RE ONLY 7 STEPS AWAY OF MOVING YOUR HOME TO THE DESTINATION OF YOUR CHOICE.

Please follow the listed 7 steps. Fill in the requested information accordingly to the form provided. Add up the WHAT MOVE FACTOR points. Add your chance. Send form. MOVE

IF HOMES DIRECT CAN'T MOVE IT, NOBODY CAN

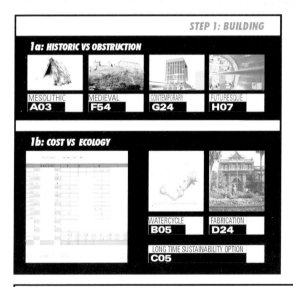

STEP 1: BUILDING

1a: HISTORIC VS OBSTRUCTION

MESOLITHIC **A03**   MEDIEVAL **F54**   CONTEMPORARY **G24**   FUTURESQUE **H07**

1b: COST VS ECOLOGY

WATERCYCLE **B05**   FABRICATION **D24**

LONG TIME SUSTAINABILITY OPTION **C05**

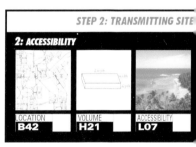

STEP 2: TRANSMITTING SITE

2: ACCESSIBILITY

LOCATION **B42**   VOLUME **H21**   ACCESSIBILITY **L07**

STEP 3: RECEIVING SITE

3: TRAVELTIME

LOCATION **A07**
PROXIMITY **A05**
OBSTACLES **B12**

Please send your payment & completed order form to: WHAT ARCHITECTURE, 1 Ravenscroft Street London E2 7SH, UK
Tel: 0044 (0) 7904 26 49 42 (ask for mail order) Fax: 0044 (0) 20 7682 0673 Email:homesdirect@whatarchitecture.com Website:www.whatarchitecture.com

HOMES DIRECT
YOUR FAVOURITE HOME DELIVERY - FOR LESS!

STEPS TO MOVE YOUR BUILDING

EE CONSULTATION   CRUISES AND TOURS   TRAVELLERS AND GIFT CHEQUES   MEMBERSHIP REWARDS -> JOIN THE IASM

END NO MONEY

HOMES DIRECT
30 - DAY FREE CREDIT ACCOUNT

We'll be glad to charge you're established 30 - DAY FREE CREDIT ACCOUNT
If you havn't set up a FREE CREDIT ACCOUNT, or prefer use your credit/debit card, please fill in below.

CREDIT CARD / DEBIT CARD
No.:

VALID FROM: EXPIRY DATE:

STEP 4: TRANSPORTATION

SIZE

GHT ESTIMATION:

% = 7175t
00142% = 100kg

MAX. WEIGHT
F60
1%
C30
0,000001%
A01

MIN. WEIGHT
B32

STEP 5: INSTALLATION

5: SERVICE AND GROUNDING

LEVELING
A11

ANCHORING
B05

INFRASTRUCTURE
D24

DISLOCATION

DISTANCE ESTIMATION:
100% = ½ WORLD CIRCUMFENCE
0,0000005% = 1,0m

100%
F60
1%
C30
0,0000005%
A01

FREE ALTITUDE TRANSFER

STEP 6: FINE TUNING

6: QUALITY ASSURANCE

WINDOWS
A07

DOORS
A05

SANITATION
B12

FREE ANGULAR REPOSITIONING IN CASE OF INSUFICIENT TV - RECEPTION

ACCESS
G31

INFRASTRUCTURE
D12

WHEATHER
C17

NEIGHBOURS
E00

MODE

2

HORSE
B26

TRUCK
B32

CRANE
C01

CHOPPER
F06

STEP 7: EXPENDITURE REPATRIATION

RECISE BALLPARK SUMMARY

IMATION OF A TYPE COST DICATORS	SUMMATION OF ALL B TYPE COST INDICATORS	SUMMATION OF ALL C TYPE COST INDICATORS	SUMMATION OF ALL D TYPE COST INDICATORS	SUMMATION OF ALL E TYPE COST INDICATORS	SUMMATION OF ALL F TYPE COST INDICATORS
	B	**C**	**D**	**E**	**F**

1000 FREE AIRMAILS BY ORDER BEFORE 12.00am

MOVE WILL BE INITIATED WITHIN 24 HOURS

. BILLING OPTIONS ARE 100% SECURE

SE ADD DESPATCH PAYMENT: Despatch charges are calculate on the net value of goods

Terms and conditions available upon request.
Prices and publication dates correct at time
of going to press but may change without notice

K/EIRE/CHANNEL ISLANDS

value up to £70.000, please add £200.00
£70.001 and £200.000, please add £300.00
en £200.000 and £400.000, please add 15%
n £400.001 and £1.000.000, please add 10%
over £1.000.001, please add 5%

EUROPE

Order value upto £75.001, please add £120.00
over £75.000 contact us for a special quotation

REST OF THE WORLD

Order value up to £30.00, please add £12.00
between £30.01 and £75.00, please add £22.00
over £75.01, please contact us for a special quotation

GATE FIVE

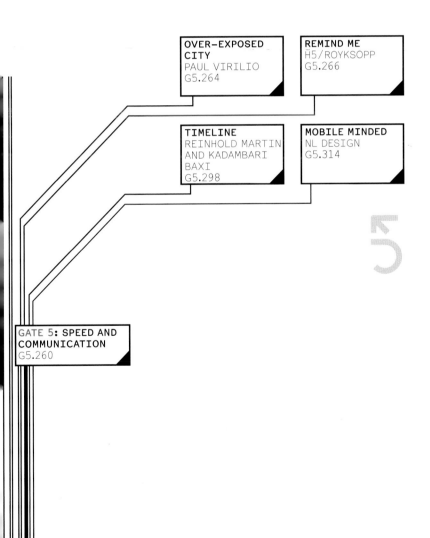

OVER—EXPOSED CITY
PAUL VIRILIO
G5.264

REMIND ME
H̄5/ROYKSOPP
G5.266

TIMELINE
REINHOLD MARTIN
AND KADAMBARI
BAXI
G5.298

MOBILE MINDED
NL DESIGN
G5.314

5

GATE 5: SPEED AND
COMMUNICATION
G5.260

speed and
communication

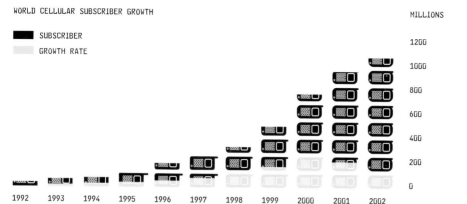

The technologies of the contemporary period embrace not only transportation but also telecommunication. Its aesthetic of mobility is the ephemera of speed and accessibility. Yet even before internet and cellular phone culture there were other modes of `modern' communication including the telegram, the telephone and the television. So why travel?

Between 1960 and 2000 the number of automobiles rose four-fold, whilst in the same period cellular phone use rose from zero to 722 million handsets.[1] At the time of printing this use had further escalated to over 1.03 billion — or 16% of listeners on earth — whilst internet traffic reports indicated 407 million web users.[2] Now that the 'modern' has been infused by the 'modem', will the singular line of history multiply and fracture into a network of simultaneity and *deja vu*: to be in two places at the same time and two times in the same place? The limits of geography and time are being obliterated.

The "Law of Proximity" posited by Paul Virilio states that in the passage from mechanical transport to the speed of present day telecommunication, the relevant unit or interval of analysis shifts from space to time and, ultimately to light.[3] In his *Overexposed City*, the city of the future is the pleasure of this interval and since this interval is light, "mechanically proximate space yields to electromagnetic proximity and the city grid to the information network; immediate practice is displaced by 'teleaction', and geopolitics by 'chronopolitics'".[4] New spaces appear, gain presence and cannibalise their predecessors in a matter of days. Mobility therefore does not demand relocation or movement of the individual: place comes to you.

Virtual travel reconfigures humans as bits of information, as individuals come to exist beyond their bodies. Given its 'instant' popularity, the need for a critical discourse on the mobile phone has arisen. In *Mobile Minded*, the need to be always switched on, always on the move, always connected means that one's existence is ultimately limited to battery life and coverage. The prolification of the phone has come at a price: semiotic pollution.

1 www.gsmworld.com/news/statistics.

2 www.gsmworld.com/news/statistics and Nua Internet Surveys, www.nua.ie.

3 Hays, K Michael, Architecture Theory Since 1968, Cambridge, Massachusetts: MIT Press, 1998, p 540.

4 Hays, Architecture Theory Since 1968.

The rapidly evolving world of the telematic will not replace the need to physically move. Travel that results in moments of physical proximity to other people, places or events remains, even today, desirable. The value of the 'face-to-face' meeting is still universally recognised; body language, voice intonation and eye contact all enable the establishment of intimacy and trust, as well as insincerity, fear, power and control in a way not possible via e-mail or phone conversation. 'Co-present interaction' is fundamental to social intercourse as a person must sense that they are close enough to be perceived in whatever they are doing, including their experiencing of others, and close enough to be perceived in this sensing of being perceived.[5] Travel, and thus proximity, remains obligatory for reasons of work, family, social intercourse and to experience spaces and events 'live'.[6]

The coupling of mechanical and digital forms of mobility mean that contemporary society is turning increasingly 'hypermobile'. Today aspatial communities are replacing geographic communities –
we spend more of our time, physically, in the midst of strangers communicating to those with which we are familiar. Whilst the benefits of mobility are widely proclaimed, hypermobility is a warning signal as to where contemporary society's fascination with 'being mobile' might take us. With this in mind, *Remind Me*, by H5, is a future memo. Presented as an infographic narrative, the lingering after-effects of today's mobile society depict a world that is immediately recognisable. Cities of suburban sprawl, diluted through cultural homogeneity – the advancement of McCulture – and functionaires who are expendable in their anonymity.

5 Boden, D and H L Molotch "The compulsion of proximity", in NowHere: Space, time and modernity, R Friedland and D Boden, eds, Berkeley: University of California Press, 1994, pp 257-86.

6 www.its.leeds.ac.uk /projects/mobilenetwo rk/downloads/urry1stp aper.doc.

the
overexposed
city
paul
virilio

At the beginning of the 1960s, with black ghettos rioting, the mayor of Philadelphia announced: "From here on in, the frontiers of the State pass to the interior of the cities." While this sentence translated the political reality for all Americans who were being discriminated against, it also pointed to an even larger dimension, given the construction of the Berlin Wall, on 13 August 1961, in the heart of the ancient capital of the Reich.

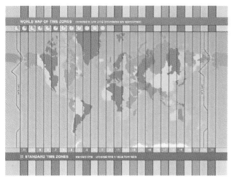

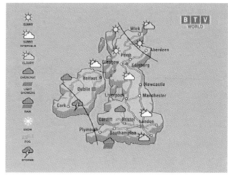

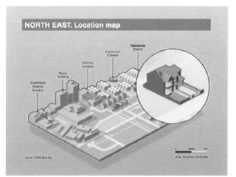

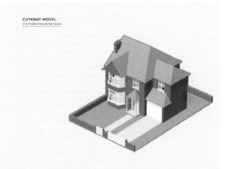

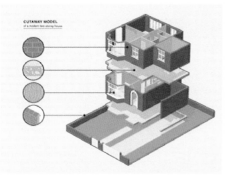

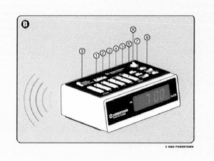

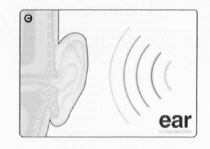

Since then, this assertion has been confirmed time and again: Belfast, Londonderry where not so long ago certain streets bore a yellow band separating the Catholic side from the Protestant, so that neither would move too far, leaving a chain-link no man's land to divide their communities even more clearly. And then there's Beirut with its East and West sections, its tortured internal boundaries, its tunnels and its mined boulevards.

Basically, the American mayor's statement revealed a general phenomenon that was just beginning to hit the capital cities as well as the provincial towns and hamlets, the phenomenon of obligatory introversion in which the City sustained the first effects of a multinational economy modelled along the lines of industrial enterprises, a real urban redeployment which soon contributed to the gutting of certain worker cities such as Liverpool and Sheffield in England, Detroit and Saint Louis in the United States, Dortmund in West Germany, and all of this at the very moment in which other areas were being built up, around tremendous international airports, a METROPLEX, a metropolitan complex such as Dallas/Fort Worth. Since the 1970s and the beginnings of the world economic crisis, the construction of these airports was further subjected to the imperatives of the defence against air pirates.

Construction no longer derived simply from traditional technical constraint. The plan had become a function of the risks of 'terrorist contamination' and the disposition of sites conceived of as sterile zones for departures and non-sterile zones for arrivals. Suddenly, all forms of loading and unloading – regardless of passenger, baggage or freight status – and all manner of airport transit

Images are stills from the video
Remind Me, by H5.

had to be submitted to a system of interior/exterior traffic control. The architecture that resulted from this had little to do with the architect's personality. It emerged instead from perceived public security requirements.

As the last gateway to the State, the airport came to resemble the fort, port or railway station of earlier days. As airports were turned into theatres of necessary regulation of exchange and communication, they also became breeding and testing grounds for high-pressured experiments in control and aerial surveillance performed for and by a new 'air and border patrol', whose anti-terrorist exploits began to make headlines with the intervention of the German GS.G9 border guards in the Mogadishu hijacking, several thousand miles away from Germany.

At that instant, the strategy of confining the sick or the suspect gave way to a tactic of mid-voyage interception. Practically, this meant examining clothing and baggage, which explains the sudden proliferation of cameras, radars and detectors in all restricted passageways. When the French built 'maximum security cell-blocks', they used the magnetised doorways that airports had had for years. Paradoxically, the equipment that ensured maximal freedom in travel formed part of the core of penitentiary incarceration. At the same time, in a number of residential areas in the United States, security was maintained exclusively through closed-circuit television hook-ups with a central police station. In banks, in supermarkets, and on major highways, where tollbooths resembled the ancient city gates, the rite of passage was no longer intermittent. It had become immanent.

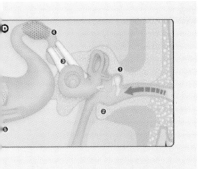

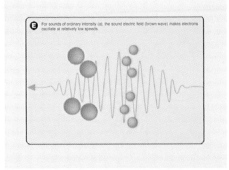

For sounds of ordinary intensity (a), the sound electric field (brown wave) makes electrons oscillate at relatively low speeds.

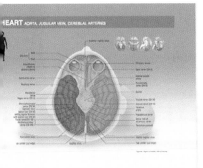

HEART AORTA, JUGULAR VEIN, CEREBRAL ARTERIES

HEART AORTA, JUGULAR VEIN, CEREBRAL ARTERIES

Like a car engine, the heart depends on electrical energy to start it and keep it beating regularly.

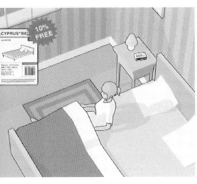

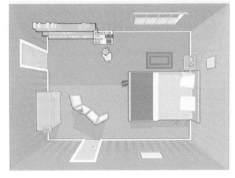

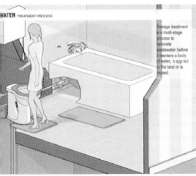

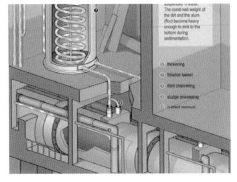

The combined weight of the dirt and the alum (floc) become heavy enough to sink to the bottom during sedimentation.

- thickening
- filtration basin
- third channeling
- sludge processing
- nutrient removal

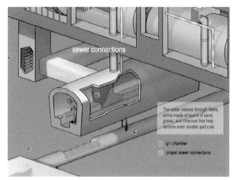

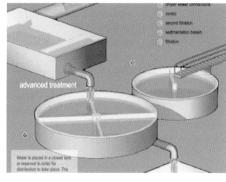

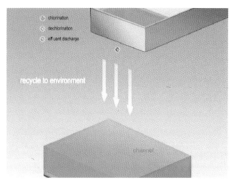

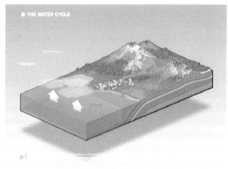

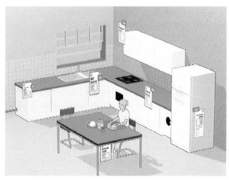

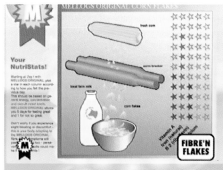

In this new perspective devoid of horizon, the city was entered not through a gate nor through an *arc de triomphe,* but rather through an electronic audience system. Users of the road were no longer understood to be inhabitants or privileged residents. They were now interlocutors in permanent transit. From this moment on, continuity no longer breaks down in space, not in the physical space of urban lots nor in the juridical space of their property tax records. From here, continuity is ruptured in time, in a time that advanced technologies and industrial redeployment incessantly arrange through a series of interruptions, such as plant closings, unemployment, casual labour and successive or simultaneous disappearing acts. These serve to organise and then disorganise the urban environment to the point of provoking the irreversible decay and degradation of neighbourhoods, as in the housing development near Lyon where the occupants' 'rate of rotation' became so great — people staying for a year and then moving on — that it contributed to the ruin of a place that each inhabitant found adequate.

In fact, since the originary enclosures, the concept of boundary has undergone numerous changes as regards both the façade and the neighbourhood it fronts. From the palisade to the screen, by way of stone ramparts, the boundary-surface has recorded innumerable perceptible and imperceptible transformations, of which the latest is probably that of the interface. Once again, we have to approach the question of access to the City in a new manner. For example, does the metropolis possess its own façade? At which moment does the city show us its face?

The phrase "to go into town", which replaced the nineteenth century's "to go to town", indicates the uncertainty of the encounter, as if we could no longer stand before the city but rather abide forever within. If the metropolis is still a place, a geographic site, it no longer has anything to do with the classical oppositions of city/country nor centre/periphery. The city is no longer organised into a localised and axial estate. While the suburbs contributed to this dissolution, in fact the intramural-extramural opposition collapsed with the transport revolutions and the development of communication and telecommunications technologies. These promoted the merger of disconnected metropolitan fringes into a single urban mass.

In effect, we are witnessing a paradoxical moment in which the opacity of building materials is reduced to zero. With the invention of the steel skeleton construction, curtain walls made of light and transparent materials, such as glass or plastics, replace stone façades, just as tracing paper, acetate and plexiglass replace the opacity of paper in the designing phase.

On the other hand, with the screen interface of computers, television and teleconferences, the surface of inscription, hitherto devoid of depth, becomes a kind of 'distance', a depth of field of a new kind of representation, a visibility without any face-to-face encounter in which the vis-a-vis of the ancient streets disappears and is erased. In this situation, a difference of position blurs into fusion and confusion. Deprived of objective boundaries, the architectonic element begins to drift and float in an electronic ether, devoid of spatial dimensions, but inscribed in the singular temporality of an instantaneous diffusion. From here on, people can't be separated by physical obstacles or by temporal distances. With the interfacing of computer terminals and video monitors, distinctions of *here* and *there* no longer mean anything.

This sudden reversion of boundaries and oppositions introduces into everyday, common space an element, which until now was reserved for the world of microscopes. There is no *plenum;* space is not filled with matter. Instead, an unbounded expanse appears in the false perspective of the machines' luminous emissions. From here on, constructed space occurs within an electronic topology where the framing of perspective and the gridwork weft of numerical images renovate the division of urban property. The ancient private/public occultation and the distinction between housing and traffic are replaced by an overexposure in which the difference between 'near' and 'far' simply ceases to exist, just as the difference between 'micro' and 'macro' vanished in the scanning of the electron microscope.

The representation of the modern city can no longer depend on the ceremonial opening of gates, nor on the ritual processions and parades lining the streets and avenues with spectators. From here on, urban architecture has to work with the opening of a new 'technological space-time'. In terms of access, telematics replaces the doorway. The sound of gates gives way to the clatter of data banks and the rites of passage of a technical culture whose progress is disguised by the immateriality of its parts and networks. Instead of operating in the space of a constructed social fabric, the intersecting and connecting grid of highway and service systems now occurs in the sequences of an imperceptible organisation of time in which the man/machine interface replaces the façades of buildings as the surfaces of property allotments.

Where once the opening of the city gates announced the alternating progression of days and nights, now we awaken to the opening of shutters and televisions. The day has been changed. A new day has been added to the astronomers' solar day, to the flickering day of candles, to the electric light. It is an electronic false-day, and it appears on a calendar of information 'commutations' that has absolutely no relationship whatsoever to real time. Chronological and historical time, time that passes, is replaced by a time that exposes itself instantaneously. On the computer screen, a time period becomes the 'support-surface' of inscription. Literally, or better cinematically, time surfaces. Thanks to the cathode-ray tube, spatial dimensions have become inseparable from their rate of transmission. As a unity of place without any unity of time, the City has disappeared into the heterogeneity of that regime comprised of the temporality of advanced technologies. The urban figure is no longer designated by a dividing line that separates here from there. Instead, it has become a computerised timetable.

Where once one necessarily entered the city by means of a physical gateway, now one passes through an audiovisual protocol in which the methods of audience and surveillance have transformed even the forms of public greeting and daily reception. Within this place of optical illusion, in which the people occupy transportation and transmission time instead of inhabiting space, inertia tends to renovate an old sedentariness, which results in the persistence of urban sites. With the new instantaneous communications media, arrival supplants departure: without necessarily leaving, everything 'arrives'.

Corn Flakes Nutrition

Calories	
Fat Calories	0
Total Fat	65 g = Less than calorie
Saturates Fat	20 g = Less than calorie
Total Carbohydrate	300 g
Dietary Fiber	25 g

FIBRE'N FLAKES

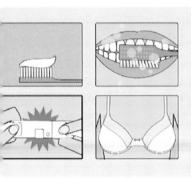

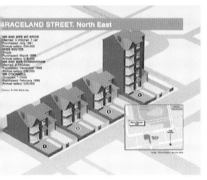

GRACELAND STREET. North East

GRACELAN

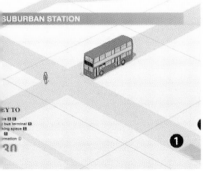

SUBURBAN STATION

KEY TO

City bus terminal
Parking space
Information

30

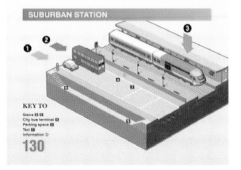

SUBURBAN STATION

KEY TO

Stairs
City bus terminal
Parking space
Taxi
Information

130

Until recently, the city separated its 'intramural'
population from those outside the walls. Today,
people are divided according to aspects of time.
Where once an entire 'downtown' area indicated a long
historical period, now only a few monuments will do.
Further, the new technological time has no relation
to any calendar of events nor to any collective
memory. It is pure computer time, and as such helps
construct a permanent present, an unbounded, timeless
intensity that is destroying the tempo of a
progressively degraded society.

What is a monument within this regime? Instead of
an intricately wrought portico or a monumental walk
punctuated by sumptuous buildings, we now have
idleness and monumental waiting for service from a
machine. Everyone is busily waiting in front of some
communications or telecommunications apparatus,
lining up at tollbooths, poring over captains'
checklists, sleeping with computer consoles on their
nightstands. Finally, the gateway is turned into a
conveyance of vehicles and vectors whose disruption
creates less a space than a countdown, in which work
occupies the centre of time while uncontrolled time
of vacations and unemployment form a periphery, the
suburbs of time, a clearing away of activities in
which each person is exiled to a life of privacy
and deprivation.

If, despite the wishes of postmodern architects, the
city from here on is deprived of gateway entries, it
is because the urban wall has long been breached by
an infinitude of openings and ruptured enclosures.
While less apparent than those of antiquity, these
are equally effective, constraining and segregating.
The illusion of the industrial revolution in
transportation misled us as to the limitlessness of

progress. Industrial time-management has imperceptibly compensated for the loss of rural territories. In the nineteenth century, the city/country attraction emptied agrarian space of its cultural and social substance. At the end of the twentieth century, urban space loses its geopolitical reality to the exclusive benefit of systems of instantaneous deportation whose technological intensity ceaselessly upsets all of our social structures. These systems include the deportation of people in the redeployment of modes of production, the deportation of attention, of the human face-to-face and the urban *vis-a-vis* encounters at the level of human/machine interaction. In effect, all of this participates in a new 'posturban' and transnational kind of concentration, as indicated by a number of recent events.

Despite the rising cost of energy, the American middle classes are evacuating the cities of the East. Following the transformation of inner cities into ghettos and slums, we now are watching the deterioration of the cities as regional centres. From Washington to Chicago, from Boston to Saint Louis, the major urban centres are shrinking. On the brink of bankruptcy, New York City lost 10% of its population in the last ten years. Meanwhile, Detroit lost 20% of its inhabitants, Cleveland 23%, Saint Louis 27%. Already, whole neighbourhoods have turned into ghost towns.

These harbingers of an imminent 'post-industrial' de-urbanisation promise an exodus that will affect all of the developed countries. Predicted for the last 40 years, this deregulation of the management of space comes from an economic and political illusion about the persistence of sites constructed in the era

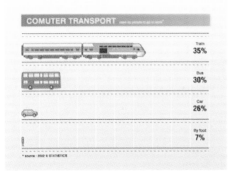

COMUTER TRANSPORT *used by people to go to work*

Train **35%**

Bus **30%**

Car **26%**

By foot **7%**

* source: 2002 © STATISTICS

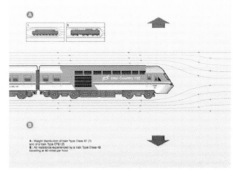

A - Weight distribution of train Type Class 97 (1) unit of 6 train Type 0781/23.
B - Air resistance experienced by a train Type Class 43 travelling at 80 miles per hour.

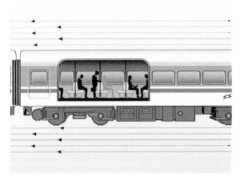

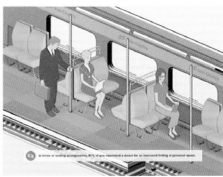

In terms of seating arrangements, 80% of you expressed a desire for an increased feeling of personal space.

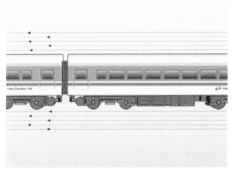

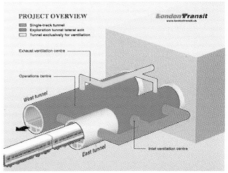

PROJECT OVERVIEW

*London**Transit***
www.londontransit.uk

Single-track tunnel
Exploration tunnel lateral exit
Tunnel exclusively for ventilation

Exhaust ventilation centre

Operations centre

West tunnel

East tunnel

Inlet ventilation centre

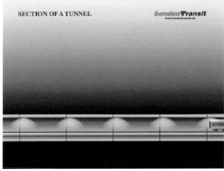

SECTION OF A TUNNEL

*London**Transit***
www.londontransit.uk

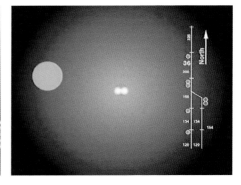

North

of automotive management of time, and in the epoch of the development of audiovisual technologies of retinal persistence.

Each surface is an interface between two environments that is ruled by a constant activity in the form of an exchange between the two substances placed in contact with one another.

This new scientific definition of surface demonstrates the contamination at work: the 'boundary, or limiting surface' has turned into an osmotic membrane, like a blotting pad. Even if this last definition is more rigorous than earlier ones, it still signals a change in the notion of limitation. The limitation of space has become commutation: the radical separation, the necessary crossing, the transit of a constant activity, the activity of incessant exchanges, the transfer between two environments and two substances. What used to be the boundary of a material, its 'terminus', has become an entryway hidden in the most imperceptible entity. From here on, the appearance of surfaces and superficies conceals a secret transparency, a thickness without thickness, a volume without volume, an imperceptible quantity.

If this situation corresponds with the physical reality of the infinitesimally small, it also fits that of the infinitely large. When what was visibly nothing becomes 'something', the greatest distance no longer precludes perception. The greatest geophysical expanse contracts as it becomes more concentrated. In the interface of the screen, everything is always already there, offered to view in the immediacy of an instantaneous transmission. In 1980, for example, when Ted Turner decided to launch

Cable News Network as a round-the-clock live news station, he transformed his subscribers' living space into a kind of global broadcast studio for world events.

Thanks to satellites, the cathode-ray window brings to each viewer the light of another day and the presence of the antipodal place. If space is that which keeps everything from occupying the same place, this abrupt confinement brings absolutely everything precisely to that 'place', that location that has no location. The exhaustion of physical, or natural, relief and of temporal distances telescopes all localisation and all position. As with live televised events, the places become interchangeable at will.

The instantaneity of ubiquity results in the atopia of a singular interface. After the spatial and temporal distances, *speed distance* obliterates the notion of physical dimension. Speed suddenly becomes a primal dimension that defies all temporal and physical measurements. This radical erasure is equivalent to a momentary inertia in the environment. The old agglomeration disappears in the intense acceleration of telecommunications, in order to give rise to a new type of concentration: the concentration of a domiciliation without domiciles, in which property boundaries, walls and fences no longer signify the permanent physical obstacle. Instead, they now form an interruption of an emission or of an electronic shadow zone which repeats the play of daylight and the shadow of buildings.

A strange topology is hidden in the obviousness of televised images. Architectural plans are displaced by the sequence plans of an invisible montage. Where geographical space once was arranged according to

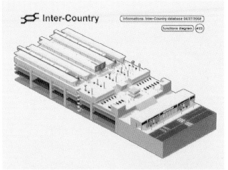

Inter-Country

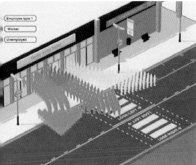

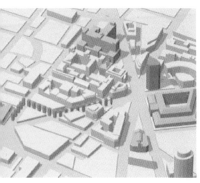
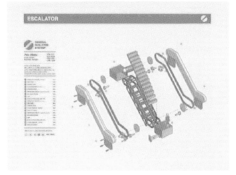

ESCALATOR

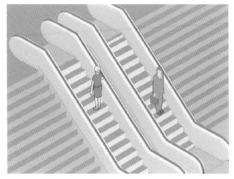

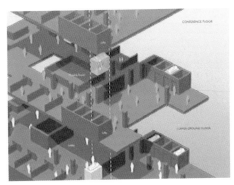
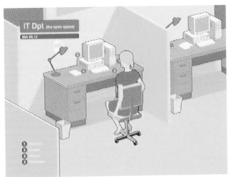

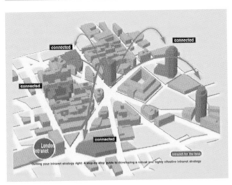
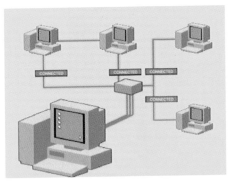
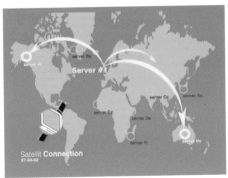
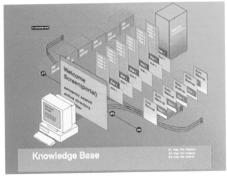

the geometry of an apparatus of rural or urban
boundary setting, time is now organised according to
imperceptible fragmentations of the technical time
span, in which the cutting, as of a momentary
interruption, replaces the lasting disappearance,
the 'programme guide' replaces the chain link fence,
just as the railroads' timetables once replaced
the almanacs.

"The camera has become our best inspector", declared
John F Kennedy, a little before being struck down in a
Dallas street. Effectively, the camera allows us to
participate in certain political and optical events.
Consider, for example, the irruption phenomenon, in
which the City allows itself to be seen thoroughly
and completely, or the diffraction phenomenon, in
which its image reverberates beyond the atmosphere
to the farthest reaches of space, while the endoscope
and the scanner allow us to see to the farthest
reaches of life.

This overexposure attracts our attention to the
extent that it offers a world without antipodes and
without hidden aspects, a world in which opacity is
but a momentary interlude. Note how the illusion of
proximity barely lasts. Where once the *polis*
inaugurated a political theatre, with its *agora* and
its *forum,* now there is only a cathode-ray screen,
where the shadows and spectres of a community dance
amid their processes of disappearance, where
cinematism broadcasts the last appearance of
urbanism, the last image of an urbanism without
urbanity. This is where tact and contact give way to
televisual impact. While tele-conferencing allows
long-distance conferences with the advantage derived
from the absence of displacement, tele-negotiating
inversely allows for the production of distance in

discussions, even when the members of the conversation are right next to each other. This is a little like those telephone crazies for whom the receiver induces flights of verbal fancy amid the anonymity of a remote control aggressiveness.

Where does the city without gates begin? Probably inside that fugitive anxiety, that shudder that seizes the minds of those who, just returning from a long vacation, contemplate the imminent encounter with mounds of unwanted mail or with a house that's been broken into and emptied of its contents. It begins with the urge to flee and escape for a second from an oppressive technological environment, to regain one's senses and one's sense of self. While spatial escape may be possible, temporal escape is not. Unless we think of layoffs as 'escape hatches', the ultimate form of paid vacation, the forward flight responds to a post-industrial illusion whose ill effects we are just beginning to feel. Already, the theory of 'job sharing' introduced to a new segment of the community – offering each person an alternative in which sharing work-time could easily lead to a whole new sharing of space as well – mirrors the rule of an endless periphery in which the homeland and the colonial settlement would replace the industrial city and its suburbs. Consider, for example, the Community Development Project, which promotes the proliferation of local development projects based on community forces, and which is intended to reincorporate the English inner cities.

Where does the edge of the exo-city begin? Where can we find the gate without a city? Probably in the new American technologies of instantaneous destruction (with explosives) of tall buildings and in the politics of systematic destruction of housing projects suddenly deemed as "unfit for the new French way of life", as in Venissieux, La Courneuve or Gagny. According to a recent French study, released by the Association for Community Development.

The destruction of 300,000 residential units over a five year period would cost 10 billion francs per year, while creating 100,000 new jobs. In addition, at the end of the demolition/reconstruction, the fiscal receipts would be 6 to 10 billion francs above the sum of public moneys invested.

One final question arises here. In a period of economic crisis, will mass destruction of the large cities replace the traditional politics of large public works? If that happens, there will be no essential difference between economic-industrial recession and war.

Architecture or post-architecture? Ultimately, the intellectual debate surrounding modernity seems part of a de-realisation phenomenon, which simultaneously involves disciplines of expression, modes of representation and modes of communication. The current wave of explosive debates within the media concerning specific political acts and their social communication now also involves the architectural expression, which cannot be removed from the world of communication systems, to the precise extent that it suffers the direct or indirect fall-out of various 'means of communication', such as the automobile or audiovisual systems.

Basically, along with construction techniques, there's always the construction of techniques, that collection of spatial and temporal mutations that is constantly reorganising both the world of everyday

experience and the aesthetic representations of
contemporary life. Constructed space, then, is more
than simply the concrete and material substance of
constructed structures, the permanence of elements
and the architectonics of urbanistic details. It also
exists as the sudden proliferation and the incessant
multiplication of special effects, which, along with
the consciousness of time and of distances, affect
the perception of the environment.

This technological deregulation of various milieux
is also topological to the exact extent that –
instead of constructing a perceptible and visible
chaos, such as the processes of degradation or
destruction implied in accident, aging and war – it
inversely and paradoxically builds an imperceptible
order, which is invisible but just as practical as
masonry or the public highways system. In all
likelihood, the essence of what we insist on calling
urbanism is composed/decomposed by these transfer,
transit and transmission systems, these transport
and transmigration networks whose immaterial
configuration reiterates the cadastral organisation
and the building of monuments.

If there are any monuments today, they are certainly
not of the visible order, despite the twists and turns
of architectural excess. No longer part of the order
of perceptible appearances nor of the aesthetic of
the apparition of volumes assembled under the sun,
this monumental disproportion now resides within the
obscure luminescence of terminals, consoles and other
electronic night-stands. Architecture is more than an
array of techniques designed to shelter us from the
storm. It is an instrument of measure, a sum total of
knowledge that, contending with the natural
environment, becomes capable of organising society's

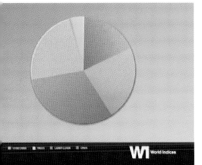

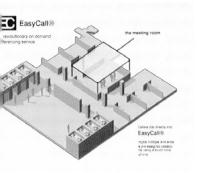

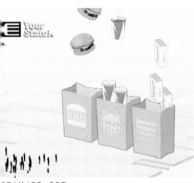

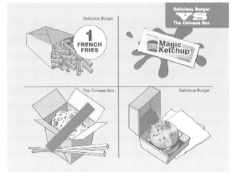

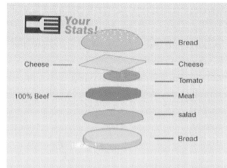

Your Stats!

- Bread
Cheese — — Cheese
— Tomato
100% Beef — — Meat
— salad
— Bread

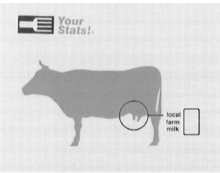

Your Stats!

local farm milk

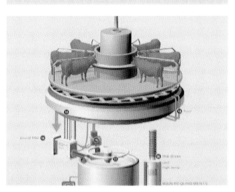

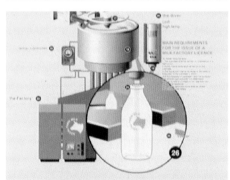

26

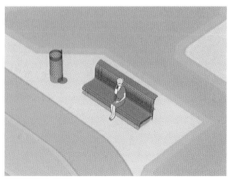

27

CLOSED

OPEN

LONDON

time and space. This geodesic capacity to define a
unity of time and place for all actions now enters
into direct conflict with the structural capacities
of the means of mass communication.

Two procedures confront each other. The first is
primarily material, constructed of physical
elements, walls, thresholds and levels, all precisely
located. The other is immaterial, and hence its
representations, images and messages afford neither
locale nor stability, since they are the vectors of a
momentary, instantaneous expression, with all the
manipulated meanings and misinformation that
presupposes.

The first one is architectonic and urbanistic in that
it organises and constructs durable geographic and
political space. The second haphazardly arranges and
deranges space-time, the continuum of societies. The
point here is not to propose a Manichaean judgment
that opposes the physical to the metaphysical, but
rather to attempt to catch the status of
contemporary, and particularly urban, architecture
within the disconcerting concert of advanced
technologies. If architectonics developed with the
rise of the City and the discovery and colonisation
of emerging lands, since the conclusion of that
conquest, architecture, like the large cities, has
rapidly declined. While continuing to invest in
internal technical equipment, architecture has
become progressively introverted, becoming a kind of
machinery gallery, a museum of sciences and
technologies, technologies derived from industrial
machinism, from the transportation revolution and
from so-called 'conquest of space'. So it makes
perfect sense that when we discuss space
technologies today, we are not referring to

architecture but rather to the engineering that
launches us into outer space.

All of this occurs as if architectonics had been
merely a subsidiary technology, surpassed by other
technologies that produced accelerated displacement
and 'sidereal' projection. In fact, this is a
question of the nature of architectural performance,
of the telluric function of the constructed realm and
the relationships between a certain cultural
technology and the earth. The development of the City
as the conservatory of classical technologies has
already contributed to the proliferation of
architecture through its projection into every
spatial direction, with the demographic
concentration and the extreme vertical densification
of the urban milieu, in direct opposition to the
agrarian model. The advanced technologies have since
continued to prolong this 'advance', through the
thoughtless and all-encompassing expansion of the
architectonic, especially with the rise of the means
of transportation.

Right now, vanguard technologies, derived from the
military conquest of space, are already launching
homes, and perhaps tomorrow the City itself, into
planetary orbit. With inhabited satellites, space
shuttles and space stations as floating laboratories
of high-tech research and industry, architecture is
flying high, with curious repercussions for the fate
of post-industrial societies, in which the cultural
markers tend to disappear progressively, what with
the decline of the arts and the slow regression of
the primary technologies.

Is urban architecture becoming an outmoded
technology, as happened to extensive agriculture,

From which came the debacles of megalopolis? Will architectonics become simply another decadent form of dominating the earth, with results like those of the uncontrolled exploitation of primary resources? Hasn't the decrease in the number of major cities already become the trope for industrial decline and forced unemployment, symbolising the failure of scientific materialism?

The recourse to History proposed by experts of postmodernity is a cheap trick that allows them to avoid the question of Time, the regime of transhistorical temporality derived from technological eco-systems. If in fact there is a crisis today, it is a crisis of ethical and aesthetic references, the inability to come to terms with events in an environment where the appearances are against us. With the growing imbalance between direct and indirect information that comes of the development of various means of communication, and its tendency to privilege information mediated to the detriment of meaning, it seems that the *reality effect* replaces immediate reality. Lyotard's modern crisis of grand narratives betrays the effect of new technologies, with the accent, from here on, placed on means more than ends.

The grand narratives of theoretical causality were thus displaced by the petty narratives of practical opportunity, and, finally, by the micro-narratives of autonomy. At issue here is no longer the 'crisis of modernity', the progressive deterioration of commonly held ideals, the proto-foundation of the meaning of History, to the benefit of more-or-less restrained narratives connected to the autonomous development of individuals. The problem now is with the narrative itself, with an official discourse or mode of representation, connected until now with the universally recognised capacity to say, describe and inscribe reality. This is the heritage of the Renaissance. Thus, the crisis in the conceptualisation of 'narrative' appears as the other side of the crisis of the conceptualisation of 'dimension' as geometrical narrative, the discourse of measurement of a reality visibly offered to all.

The crisis of the grand narrative that gives rise to the micro-narrative finally becomes the crisis of the narrative of the grand and the petty.

This marks the advent of a disinformation in which excess and incommensurability are, for 'postmodernity', what the philosophical resolution of problems and the resolution of the pictorial and architectural image were to the birth of the Enlightenment.

The crisis in the conceptualisation of dimension becomes the crisis of the whole.

In other words, the substantial, homogeneous space derived from classical Greek geometry gives way to an accidental, heterogeneous space in which sections and fractions become essential once more. Just as the land suffered the mechanisation of agriculture, urban topography has continuously paid the price for the atomisation and disintegration of surfaces and of all references that tend towards all kinds of transmigrations and transformations. This sudden exploding of whole forms, this destruction of the properties of the individual by industrialisation, is felt less in the city's space – despite the dissolution of the suburbs – than in the time – understood as sequential perceptions – of urban

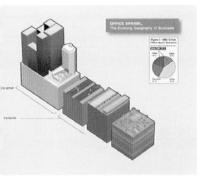
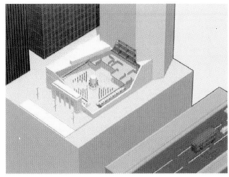
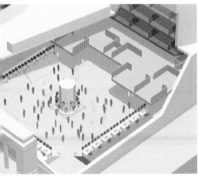
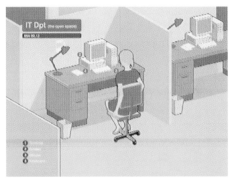

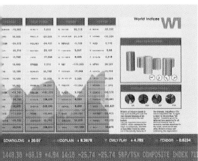

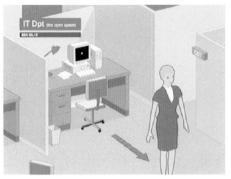

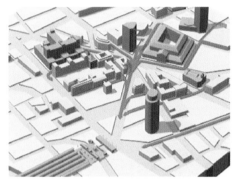
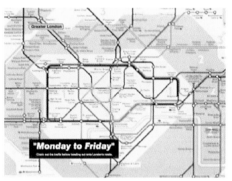
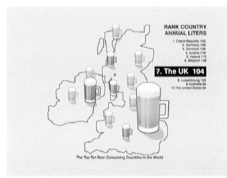

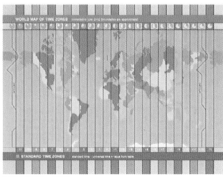
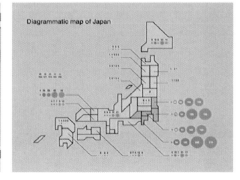

appearances. In fact, transparency has long
supplanted appearances. Since the beginning of the
twentieth century, the classical depth of field has
been revitalised by the depth of time of advanced
technologies. Both the film and aeronautics
industries took off soon after the ground was broken
for the grand boulevards. The parades on Haussmann
Boulevard gave way to the Lumiere brothers'
accelerated motion picture inventions; the esplanades
of Les Invalides gave way to the invalidation of the
city plan. The screen abruptly became the city square,
the crossroads of all mass media.

From the aesthetics of the appearance of a *stable*
image – present as an aspect of its static nature –
to the aesthetics of the disappearance of an *unstable*
image – present in its cinematic and cinematographic
flight of escape – we have witnessed a transmutation
of representations. The emergence of forms as volumes
destined to persist as long as their materials would
allow has given way to images whose duration is
purely retinal. So, more than Venturi's Las Vegas, it
is Hollywood that merits urbanist scholarship, for,
after the theatre cities of Antiquity and of the
Italian Renaissance, it was Hollywood that was the
first Cinecitta, the city of living cinema where
stage-sets and reality, tax-plans and scripts, the
living and the living dead, mix and merge
deliriously.

Here more than anywhere else advanced technologies
combined to form a synthetic space-time.

Babylon of filmic de-formation, industrial zone of
pretence, Hollywood was built neighbourhood by
neighbourhood, block by block, on the twilight of
appearances, the success of magicians' tricks, the

rise of epic productions like those of DW Griffith, all the while waiting for the megalomaniacal urbanisations of Disneyland, Disney World and Epcot Center. When Francis Ford Coppola, in *One From the Heart,* electronically inlaid his actors into a life-size Las Vegas built at the Zoetrope studios in Hollywood (simply because the director wanted the city to adapt to his shooting schedule instead of the other way around), he overpowered Venturi, not by demonstrating the ambiguities of contemporary architecture, but by showing the 'spectral' characters of the city and its denizens.

The utopian 'architecture on paper' of the 1960s took on the video-electronic special effects of people like Harryhausen and Tumbull, just at the precise instant that computer screens started popping up in architectural firms. "Video doesn't mean I see; it means I fly", according to Nam June Paik. With this technology, the 'aerial view' no longer involves the theoretical altitudes of scale models. It has become an opto-electronic interface operating in real time, with all that this implies for the redefinition of the image. If aviation – appearing the same year as cinematography – entailed a revision of point of view and a radical mutation of our perception of the world, infographic technologies will likewise force a readjustment of reality and its representations. We already see this in 'Tactical Mapping Systems', a video-disc produced by the United States Defence Department's Agency for Advanced Research Projects. This system offers a continuous view of Aspen, Colorado, by accelerating or decelerating the speed of 54,000 images, changing direction or season as easily as one switches television channels, turning the town into a kind of shooting gallery in which the functions of eyesight and weaponry melt into each other.

If architectonics once measured itself according to geology, according to the tectonics of natural reliefs, with pyramids, towers and other neo-gothic tricks, today it measures itself according to state-of-the-art technologies, whose vertiginous prowess exiles all of us from the terrestrial horizon.

Neo-geological, the 'Monument Valley' of some pseudo-lithic era, today's metropolis is a phantom landscape, the fossil of past societies whose technologies were intimately aligned with the visible transformation of matter, a project from which the sciences have increasingly turned away.

Sources

Adorno, Theodor, "Functionalism Today", trans Jane Newman and John Smith, Oppositions, no 17, Summer 1979, pp 30-41.

Bataille, Georges, "Architecture", "Museum", "Slaughterhouse", trans Paul Hegarty. Originally published as: "Architecture", Dictionnaire Critique, 1929, 2, p 117; "Musee", Dictionnaire Critique, 1930, 5, p 300; "Abattoir", Dictionnaire Critique, 1929, 6, p 329.

Benjamin, Walter, "On Some Motifs in Baudelaire", Illuminations, trans Harry Zohn, London: Fontana, 1973, Sections 5-8, pp 162-72.

Benjamin, Walter, "Paris, Capital of the Nineteenth Century", Reflections, trans. Edmund Jephcott, New York, London: Harcourt Brace Jovanovich, 1978, Sections 1, 4, 5, 6; pp 146-149; 154-162.

Bloch, Ernst, "Formative Education, Engineering Form, Ornament", trans Jane Newman and John Smith, Oppositions, no 17, Summer 1979, pp 45-51.

Kracauer, Siegfried, "The Hotel Lobby" (extract), Mass Ornament, trans Thomas Levin, Cambridge, MA: Harvard University Press, 1995.

timeline reinhold martin and kadambari baxi

Timeline is a multi-part project that passes through the recent past and the not-too-distant future. Its primary purpose is to rethink the city without remorse, and thus to rethink architecture in a globalised, digital age.

About Time

Northern California's Silicon Valley has long been a laboratory from which 'the future' has been launched. *Timeline* follows suit, but paradoxically – by bending the arrow of techno-economic 'progress' into a circle: the future as feedback loop. Only by inducing a certain vertigo, a certain *temporal disequilibrium* (as in: running around in circles), might it be possible to break out of the closed loops in which our technologies and our economies lock us, all of us. The largest of these loops is called the 'globe'.

Global Village-machine

Where it once may have seemed enough to encourage both architecture and its users to propel themselves along trajectories, to fling themselves onto vectors, this path has reached a dead end or really, a cul-de-sac, since globalisation always recaptures these lines and

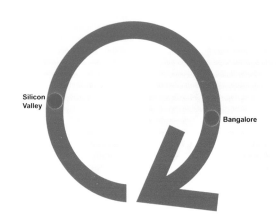

Silicon Valley

Bangalore

pulls them back in. For example, in the relentlessly circular 'global village' the distance (geographic, cultural, economic, technological) between Silicon Valley in northern California, and Bangalore in southern India is not so much collapsed as fed back into itself in a 24/7 work cycle. While well-paid programmers in Silicon Valley sleep, less well-paid programmers in Bangalore's 'body shops' tap the keys. Returning to work after their morning commute, the Californians (significant percentages of whom hail from South Asia) find new code on their desktops. Around it goes, in circles.

Thus, the faster things go (approaching the speed of light along thousands of miles of fibre-optic cable), the more integrated this village-machine becomes. There is no escape velocity to be attained here, except in the paradoxical sense of *accelerating* the tendency toward entropy inherent in this process by running faster and faster in circles. This is the sense in which the evolutionary timeline laid out here is first circular and ultimately, nonlinear.

Movement
Remember the 'modern movement'? Today, everybody's still on the move, apparently. But where are they all going? Scurrying about like rats in a cage, little dots connected by dotted lines in digital diagrams.

History 101
Highway 101, a central artery running through Silicon Valley, offers a path through which to rethink architecture's presumed mobility and its movements — modern or otherwise. And so we take a drive into the recent past and the near future. Into the parking lots and cul-de-sacs of time.

In the Round

Imagine a house located in the centre of a circular plot
of land. A whole neighbourhood of houses located in the
centres of circular plots of land. Imagine the mowing
patterns: around and around the lawn, in circles. Going
nowhere. Except for the driveway, and with it, the grand
interruption of the car. When people get into their
cars, they go places. The car is, after all, the very
emblem of the 'modern movement' (recall: machine-à-
habiter). It is the very emblem of going places, of
progress, of the future.

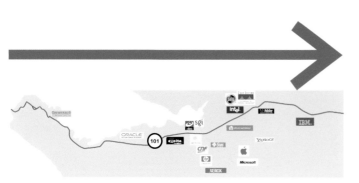

Traffic

Driving along Highway 101, it's not very obvious that
the car has been replaced with another machine as
instrument and emblem of progress. But the evidence is
there if you look. It's there, for instance, in the logos
attached to the buildings, sometimes visible from the
highway, sometimes from the side streets. Oracle, Excite,
Intel, Silicon Graphics, CNF, Hewlett-Packard, Sun, Palm,
Applied Materials, Genentech, Xerox, Alza, Adobe, Yahoo!,
Microsoft, Agilent, Apple, IBM, Cisco Systems…. These are
road signs, arrows pointing toward the future. Some have
already disappeared.

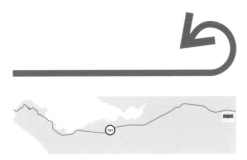

It is possible to drive south along this Information
Highway and follow the arrow of progress, from Palo Alto
(and the Stanford Industrial Park) to San Jose (and the
new monuments of the 'new economy'). Unless, of course,
you get stuck in traffic.

Coyote Valley

If you make it to the end of the arrow, to the very tip,
the cutting edge, the vanguard, the avant-garde, you
will have arrived at Coyote Valley, a Silicon Valley-in-
miniature, and a terminus for other dreams from other
times. It is a bottleneck in time, a point at which
progress (or "movement") gets stuck in traffic and
bends its arrow into a feedback loop.

1964: Oceanic California, a subsidiary of Castle & Cooke, plans "New Town San Jose" in Coyote Valley. The project is abandoned.

1984: Tandem scheduled to begin campus in Coyote Valley. Plans are abandoned.

1985: Apple announces plan to build world headquarters in Coyote Valley site. The project is abandoned.

2000: Cisco Systems announces Coyote Valley as site for new campus for 20,000 worker-consumers. Design: Devcon Construction. Plans put on hold.

2001: Martin/Baxi Architects borrow the Cisco project. Plans in progress.

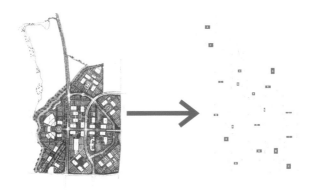

By the Numbers

2000

Cisco Systems, Inc. and Devcon Construction propose a
major new office complex organised around the
automobile in the Coyote Valley Research Park in south
San Jose, California.

Total area:	6.6 million s.f.	Floor Area Ratio:	.25
Employees:	20,000	Maximum height:	8 stories
Buildings:	38	Configuration:	Village
Character:	Virtually identical		

2001

Martin/Baxi Architects propose a major new office
complex organised around the *computer* in the Coyote
Valley Research Park in south San Jose, California.

Total area:	6.6 million s.f.	Floor Area Ratio:	.5
Employees:	20,000	Maximum height:	24 stories
Buildings:	19	Configuration:	Scatter
Character:	Endlessly different yet endlessly similar		

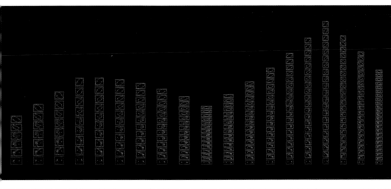

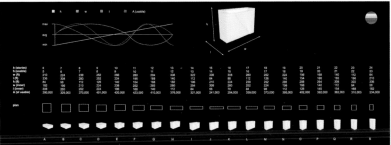

The iMac Principle

Think different.
Every building, different.
Every floor of every building, different.
Every column of every floor of every building,
different.
Same difference.

This parametric principle combines a range of variables
– height, width, length, size of atrium – into 19
prototypical office blocks. The result is a 'timeline'
of different-sized buildings that encapsulates *in situ*
the transition (already under way in Silicon Valley)
from predominantly low 'pancake' buildings to taller
towers, as land values and densities increase.

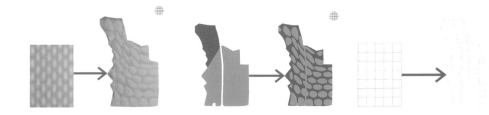

The Atrium Principle

Each of these buildings is trapped in its own atrium. A volume of flexible office space is encapsulated in an artificial environment, an atrium, which also infiltrates it from within, introducing a vortex of pseudo-public space through the centre of the volume. The deepest interior of the office is thus invaded by other programmes – food courts, shopping, services, leisure – that are increasingly typical of a corporate lifestyle in which work and living become indistinguishable. The surrounding atrium also functions as a breathable, environmentally progressive double skin that nonetheless seals off the workplace in a self-contained, artificial vitrine.

This is the space of 'the computer', a continuous interior, a micro-world of flexible worktimes and user-friendly sociability. A whole host of pseudo-freedoms converge in the scene of happy workers attached to wireless networks while consuming ethnically diverse lunches in the food courts of the global corporation. Cisco calls its worker-friendly managerial philosophy "The Cisco Way". We only propose a generalisation. Where the iMac Principle systematises consumerist 'choice' in a smooth, quantitative gradient, The Atrium Principle further softens the authoritarian edges of the corporate workspace with a soothing gradient of lifestyle supplements – services and amenities provided free of charge by a benevolent institution in the interest of total integration. There is no outside to the corporate lifestyle, only a range of choices within it.

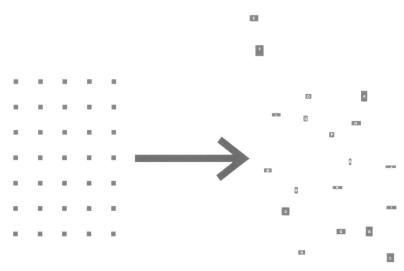

Scatter

How do these inward looking office machines relate to each other? How do these monuments to consumerist isolation connect, if at all? Like the corporate subjects they serve, they are, in fact, invisibly networked together, but not in a linear chain or in a surging, multiplicitous force-field. Instead, they are scattered in their own circularity. Each object, swirling around a vortex of internal differentiation, of endless choices, spins off erratically and

unpredictably, further detaching itself from all overt
linkages, all causal chains, all determinate vectors,
all progressive arrows.

Thus we continue to seek out the entropic, the flat — the
undifferentiated and the hyper-differentiated — in order
to feed it back into itself. But even Silicon Valley is
not flat enough. Its corporate landscape still clings to
hierarchies, grand axial approaches, lobbies and
boardrooms that resist the absolute interchangeability
heralded by The iMac Principle. And so, The Golf Course
Principle works to flatten things out further by
redistributing this landscape and its resources — both
natural and artificial — into an undulating network of
isolated points. Another gradient is installed, ranging
from "green" (fully manicured lawns at the high points)
to "rough" (unmanaged, indigenous growth at the low),
in the manner of a golf course. An even grid of such
mounds and valleys is stretched into the uneven outline
of the site, resulting in a gradient of mound sizes.
Overlaid on this is a grid of property lines, stretched
unevenly across the site, resulting in a gradient of
subdivisions, with lot sizes ranging from maximum to
minimum.

Each plot in the site plan is thereby differentiated
quantitatively (and qualitatively) from all the others
by virtue of its position, size, configuration, contour,
and hence, buildable area. Hence, each quantitatively
(and qualitatively) unique building can now be matched
with a compatible and quantitatively unique plot, and
located accordingly. Call the whole thing The Cisco
System. The low-to-high timeline — the arrow of
progress, again — thus spins out into an apparently
random scatter. Entropy.

The Entropy Principle (Estrangement, Again)

A new kind of city is thus incubated in this scatter
and projected backward into Silicon Valley along its
highways, accelerating its tendency toward entropy while
also multiplying its density. A familiar strangeness and
a dense emptiness are its greatest assets. Since it is
not that ex-urban sprawl and a corporate lifestyle are
alienating, it is that they are not alienating enough. To
manage their dislocations, both actively seek out
integration into the greater whole of the village —
suburban, corporate, or global — in the interest of
maximum performance with a minimum of dissent.

In contrast The Entropy Principle, the generalisation
of all the other Principles enumerated above, offers a
counter-future to that projected by the values of
'consumer confidence' and technologicalprogress.com.
Here, hiding in cul-de-sacs, in atriums, in golf courses,

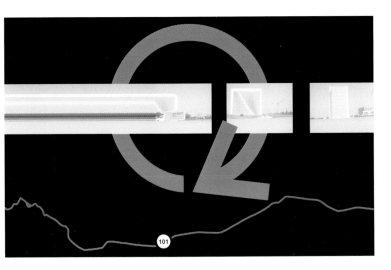

and in a host of other 'technologies', is a new form of
urbanity that looks back on the modern metropolis — the
city of strangers — with a fond respect, while looking
forward toward a strangely familiar future that remains
a work in progress. It has been almost 100 years since
the archetypal subject of that metropolis was
discovered: The Stranger, cousin to the aimless,
streetwalking flâneur. Now, with the lapse of the modern
period, it is possible that the archetypal subject of
the new post-metropolis is The Resident Alien, a subject
on the run but stuck in traffic, going nowhere in
particular, but not quite standing still.

mobile
minded
nt design

Mobile networks have to negotiate the architecture of spaces that they attempt to inhabit. Although the interfaces have removed themselves from physical architectures, the radio waves that connect cell spaces are refracted and reflected by these same obstacles, creating not a seamless network but a series of ebbs and flows. The supposedly flat surface of the network is in fact warped, pulled into troughs and peaks by the gravity of architecture and the users themselves.

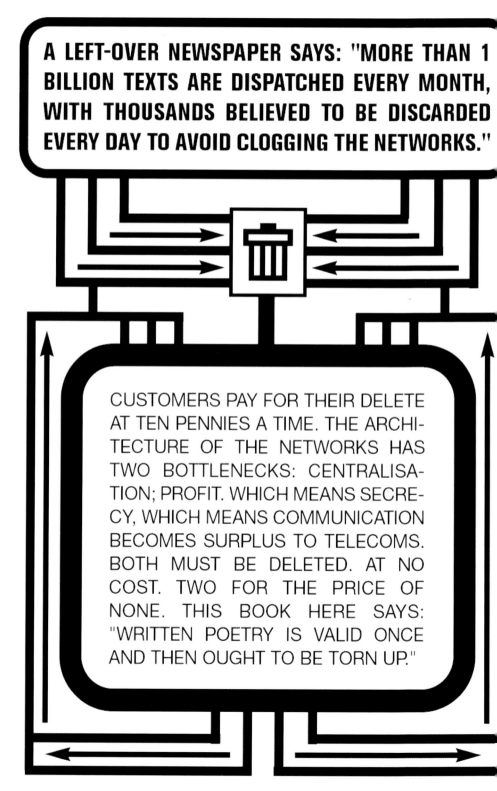

A LEFT-OVER NEWSPAPER SAYS: "MORE THAN 1 BILLION TEXTS ARE DISPATCHED EVERY MONTH, WITH THOUSANDS BELIEVED TO BE DISCARDED EVERY DAY TO AVOID CLOGGING THE NETWORKS."

CUSTOMERS PAY FOR THEIR DELETE AT TEN PENNIES A TIME. THE ARCHITECTURE OF THE NETWORKS HAS TWO BOTTLENECKS: CENTRALISATION; PROFIT. WHICH MEANS SECRECY, WHICH MEANS COMMUNICATION BECOMES SURPLUS TO TELECOMS. BOTH MUST BE DELETED. AT NO COST. TWO FOR THE PRICE OF NONE. THIS BOOK HERE SAYS: "WRITTEN POETRY IS VALID ONCE AND THEN OUGHT TO BE TORN UP."

PUT YOUR LIFE NEVER INTO THE HANDS OF A BATTERY

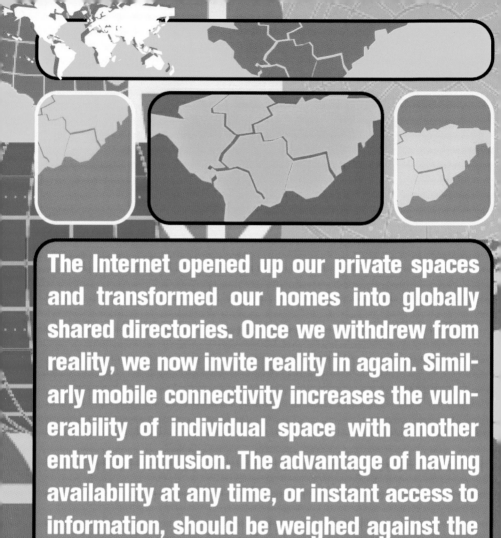

The Internet opened up our private spaces and transformed our homes into globally shared directories. Once we withdrew from reality, we now invite reality in again. Similarly mobile connectivity increases the vulnerability of individual space with another entry for intrusion. The advantage of having availability at any time, or instant access to information, should be weighed against the disadvantages of these dependencies.

obile phones enable the type of (virtual) communication and interaction hich characterizes premodernity:

eople who never move far, ve in small towns and illages near each other, everybody knows here everybody is etc.

ut being virtual, this kind of communi-cation is not bounding more to any ngle locality, as it was in premodern mes. This makes it a very postmod-rn phenomenon.

lobile phones make it possible to mpirically test some of the claims ade by postmodern authors. And at is defenitly why the subject as been so meticulously avoided.

P. Roos, Postmodernity and Mobile Communications
tp://www.valt.helsinki.fi/staff/jproos/mobilezation.htm)

WHERE ONCE WE BOUGHT GROUND OR CLAIMED RIGHTS IN EXTRA-TERRITORIAL WATERS, WITH RADIO, TELEPHONY, AIRTRAVEL AND TV AN IMMENSE TRADE IN AIR HAS ARISEN. WAVE FREQUENCIES, AIR ROUTES, AND THE SPACE ABOVE APARTMENT BUILDINGS ARE THE 'GOODS' OF SPECULATIVE TRADE. THE FURTHEST FRONT LINES IN THIS AIR WAR, THAT BEGUN IN WORLD WAR I, HAVE NOW MOVED TO THE UMTC FREQUENCIES THAT PUT POCKET-SIZE INTERNET WITHIN REACH.

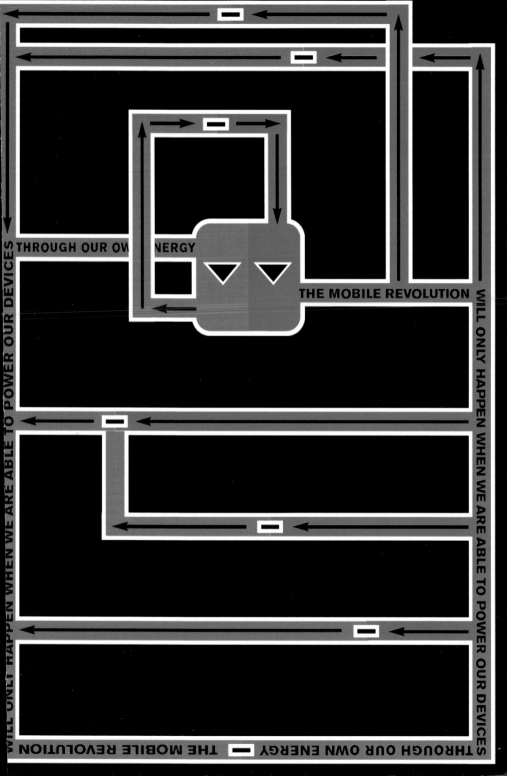

contributors

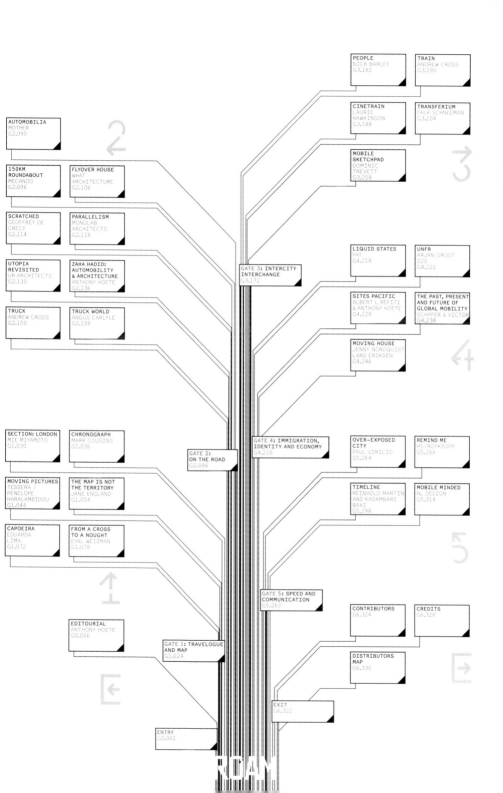

AUTOMOBILIA
MOTHER
G2.090

150KM ROUNDABOUT
MECANOO
G2.096

FLYOVER HOUSE
WHAT ARCHITECTURE
G2.106

SCRATCHED
GEOFFREY DE CRECY
G2.114

PARALLELISM
MONOLAB ARCHITECTS
G2.118

UTOPIA REVISITED
UR ARCHITECTS
G2.130

ZAHA HADID: AUTOMOBILITY & ARCHITECTURE
ANTHONY HOETE
G2.136

TRUCK
ANDREW CROSS
G2.150

TRUCK WORLD
ANGUS CARLYLE
G2.158

PEOPLE
NICK BARLEY
G3.182

TRAIN
ANDREW CROSS
G3.190

CINETRAIN
LAURIE HAWKINSON
G3.188

TRANSFERIUM
FALK SCHNEEMAN
G3.204

MOBILE SKETCHPAD
DOMINIC TREVETT
G3.208

GATE 3: INTERCITY INTERCHANGE
G3.172

LIQUID STATES
FAT
G4.218

UNFR
ARJAN GROOT
O2O
G4.222

SITES PACIFIC
ALBERT L REFITI & ANTHONY HOETE
G4.228

THE PAST, PRESENT AND FUTURE OF GLOBAL MOBILITY
SCHAFER & VICTOR
G4.238

MOVING HOUSE
JENNY NORDQUIST
LARS ERIKSEN
G4.246

SECTION: LONDON
MIE MIYAMOTO
G1.030

CHRONOGRAPH
MARK COUSINS
G1.036

MOVING PICTURES
TESSERA / PENELOPE HARALAMBIDOU
G1.044

THE MAP IS NOT THE TERRITORY
JANE ENGLAND
G1.054

CAPOEIRA
EDUARDA LIMA
G1.072

FROM A CROSS TO A NOUGHT
EYAL WEIZMAN
G1.078

GATE 2: ON THE ROAD
G2.086

GATE 4: IMMIGRATION, IDENTITY AND ECONOMY
G4.216

OVER-EXPOSED CITY
PAUL VIRILIO
G5.264

REMIND ME
H5/ROYKSOPP
G5.266

TIMELINE
REINHOLD MARTIN AND KADAMBARI BAXI
G5.298

MOBILE MINDED
NL DESIGN
G5.314

GATE 5: SPEED AND COMMUNICATION
G5.260

CONTRIBUTORS
G6.324

CREDITS
G6.328

DISTRIBUTORS MAP
G6.330

EDITOURIAL
ANTHONY HOETE
G0.006

GATE 1: TRAVELOGUE AND MAP
G1.024

EXIT
G6.322

ENTRY
G0.001

RDAM

MIE MIYAMOTO

Mie Miyamoto studied at both the
Architecture Association, School
of Architecture and the Bartlett
School of Architecture, London
and was awarded a 2 year
scholarship to undertake the
project Section: London.
mie_miyamoto@yahoo.co.jp

MARK COUSINS

Mark Cousins is Director of
General Studies and the Histories
and Theories Graduate Programme
at the Architectural Association.
A founder member of the new
graduate school The London
Consortium and visiting Professor
of Architecture at Columbia
University, New York.

TESSERA

Tessera is a collaborative
architectural practice founded in
1999 by Anthony Boulanger,
Penelope Haralambidou, Yeoryia
Manolopoulou and Eduardo Rosa.
The team is involved in practice,
research and theory intersecting
architecture and the visual arts,
and their projects reflect on
issues addressing contemporary
public space. Tessera has taken
part in international
competitions and exhibitions and
their work has been published in
Greece, France and Britain.
Tessera has been recently
appointed by the Hellenic
Ministry of Culture to design the
exhibition 'Metabolics: Athens-
scape for the 2004 Olympics', to
take place at the RIBA London in
April 2003.
haralambidou@btinternet.com

ENGLAND + CO

Jane England is the director of
England & Co Gallery in Notting
Hill, London. Initially trained
as an art historian, she founded
the gallery in 1987 and has
curated numerous exhibitions of
contemporary art and artists, as
well as an ongoing series of
retrospective exhibitions re-
appraising art and artists from
the avant garde of the second
half of the twentieth century.
england.gallery@virgin.net

EDUARDA LIMA

Portugese Editorial Assistant
to ROAM.
e_lima22@yahoo.co.uk

MOTHER

Mother is a London Ad Agency who
launched in 1996 with Channel 5.
Other accounts include E-map,
Coca-cola, Siemens, Egg and
memorably ITV with its monkey
moniker that inspired new levels
of celebrity bestiality.
www.motherlondon.com

MECANOO

www.mecanoo.nl

EYAL WEIZMAN

Eyal Weizman, AA Dip, is an
Israeli architect and critic
working in London and Tel Aviv.
He taught architecture at the
University of Applied Arts in
Vienna, the Technion in Israel
the NIA in Rotterdam and the
Bartlett School of Architecture.
He is undertaking research at the
London Consortium and is
currently working on a report for
the Israeli organisation B'tselem
on human-rights violation through
the use of planning and
architecture in the West Bank.
eyal@eruv.net

GEOFFREY DE CRECY

Geoffrey de Crecy uses the language of video games in his animations. The promotional video for "Scratched" was for his 'house artist' brother Etienne de Crecy's (Motorbass, Cassius et al) album Tempovision. This treatise on the automobile and the city is reminiscent of the painter de Chirico's vacated urbanism: two urban youths patrol a vacant cityscape in search of electricity.

MONOLAB

Monolab, founded in 1999, declares "Simplicity (MONO) linked to experiment (LAB). The main target of the office is to create chances and opportunities to solve complex urban and architectural issues by investing extra energy during the conceptual phase of the process; the phases in which the most important, determinant, final and radical decisions are taken." mail@monolab.nl

UR ARCHITECTS

The winning of the architectural competition Europan 6 (Lelystad site) led to the formation of UR architects: Regis Verplaetse, Chris Burton, Eddy Joaquim and Nikolaas Vande Keere. After this success, the office were asked by the municipality of Lelystad to carry out a follow-up study into the feasibility of the competition concept 'Utopia Revisited'.
ur_architects@mail.com

ZAHA HADID ARCHITECTS

Zaha Hadid is an architect who consistently shifts the boundaries of architecture and urban design. Her work experiments with spatial quality, extending and intensifying existing landscapes in the pursuit of a visionary aesthetic that encompasses all fields of design, ranging from urban scale through to products, interiors and furniture. Best known for her seminal built works (Vitra Fire Station, Land Fomation-One and the Strasbourg Tram Station) her central concerns involve a simultaneous engagement in practice, teaching and research.
www.zaha-hadid.com

ANDREW CROSS

Andrew Cross is a photographer and curator. His book Some Trains In America is published by Prestel. His Year of The Artist residency was hosted by Swindon Borough Council and English Heritage/National Monuments Record Centre.
www.andrewcross.com

ANGUS CARLYLE

Dr Angus Carlyle is a Senior Lecturer in Sound Art and Design at the London College of Printing. He was the editor of the fashion and culture magazine, themepark, and has contributed to a variety of publications, from The Journal of Political Studies, through art exhibition catalogues and on to books on architecture, photography and philosophical suicides. He is currently completing a book about the art-pop band, The KLF, to be released in summer 2003. He entertains intermittent fantasies of jacking it all in, buying a Winnebago Le Sharo and pursuing, with his family, the aesthetics of mobility across Europe's northern shores.

NICK BARLEY
Nick Barley is the author/editor
of a number of publications
including Breathing Cities, City
Levels and Lost and Found.
nbarley@augustmedia.co.uk

LAURIE HAWKINSON
The architecture of Smith-Miller
+ Hawkinson, New York embodies a
profound respect for the
tradition of Modern Architecture,
for it has a compelling substance
which is spatially innovative,
enriched by attention to place,
cognizant of use, materiality and
human scale. Their buildings
contribute to society and speak
in an innovative language to the
art of architecture.

FALK SCHNEEMAN
Falk Schneeman is a final year
student and a member of the
Aesthetic of Mobility atelier
taught by Anthony Hoete and
Francine Houben at the Technical
University of Delft in the
Netherlands.
fschneemann@yahoo.de

DOMINIC TREVETT
dominictrevett@btinternet.com

FAT
Fat is a company that makes
architecture and art (and all
kinds of things in between). We
are interested in making work
that explores the experiences,
contradictions and possibilities
of the modern world. Charting a
course that engages creatively
with the choppy waters of
commerce – finding tactics and
solutions that are simultaneously
conceptually interesting,
culturally relevant, and
aesthetically engaging. Most
importantly we work in the
culture bunker, rather than the
ivory tower.
www.fat.co.uk

ARJAN GROOT / 020
www.nultwintig.com

ALBERT REFITI
Architect and cultural theorist,
Albert Refiti is a lecturer in
Spatial Design at the Auckland
University of Technology School
of Arts and Design. In
collaboration with Anthony Hoete,
he is formalising and editing the
publication Sites Pacific: a
charting of the locational
conditions specific to the South
Pacific that inform local
cultural practices such as
architecture and suburbanism.
albert.refiti@aut.ac.nz

ANDREAS SCHAFER
Schafer and Victor collaborate on
long-term and large-scale models
of transportation. Schafer, an
aeronautical engineer, works at
the MIT Centre for Technology,
Policy and Industrial Development
on systems analysis on
transportation and global change.

DAVID VICTOR
Victor is working on the
Environmentally Compatible Energy
Strategies Project at the
International Institute for
Applied Systems Analysis focusing
on energy technology and
international environmental
guidance.

JENNY NORDQUIST
Photographer for "Moving House".
www.jennynordquist.com
mail@jennynordquist.com

LARS ERIKSEN
Writer for "Moving House".
lars@hinnerskov.co.uk

PAUL VIRILIO

Paul Virilio is one of the most significant French cultural theorists writing today. Increasingly hailed as the inventor of concepts such as 'dromology' (the 'science' of speed), Virilio is renowned for his declaration that the logic of acceleration lies at the heart of the organisation and transformation of the modern world. Virilio suggests that, today, all cities are overexposed.

MARTIN/BAXI

Kadambari Baxi is a partner with Martin/Baxi Architects and a principal of imageMachine [multimedia design]. Her architectural practice consists of experimental as well commissioned projects. Reinhold Martin is an Assistant Professor of Architecture at Columbia University and is an editor of the journal Grey Room. He is the co-author, with Baxi, of Entropia (London: Black Dog Publishing, 2001) documenting their collaborative work; and his book, The Organizational Complex: Architecture, Media, and Corporate Space is forthcoming in 2003.
baxi@imagemachine.com

NL DESIGN

NL Design is a company permanently under construction. It is a work in progress without a business plan. In the future, it will be an organisation or platform where designers can discuss; they can use it to create and show new and develop new visions in the world of design. And since is everything, this is becoming a wide area.
www.nl-design.tv

H5

Antoine Bardou-Jacquet operates a graphic design studio, H5, in the same offices as Paris-based record label Solid. Having dwelled on the idea of using typography and words to convey a more visual meaning for some time, Bardou-Jacquet implemented this concept with a music video for Alex Gopher's song "The Child". Set in NYC, the video follows a young couple rushing through the city to reach the hospital to have their baby delivered. The streets, buildings (the Guggenheim Museum), people and the couple themselves are visually represented by type-the viewer is left able to interpret the meaning of these words.
hcino@wanadoo.fr

LASZLO FECSKE

Hungarian Editorial Assitant to ROAM.
laszlo@macmail.com

ANTHONY HOETE

Maori Patuwai o Ngati Awa, New Zealand passport holder, Dutch Architectural registration, private pilot's Licence, Belgian wife, Italian daughter, living in London. Teaches Spatial Mobility at the Technical University of Delft. Established WHAT Architecture in 2000.
info@whatarchitecture.com

WHAT ARCHITECTURE

WHAT Architecture (Anthony Hoete and Alar Jost) is a practice without an office. The city is today characterised by an immense instability caused by flow and friction: the transience of its demographic, the exchange of goods and services, the sensitising resonance between phenomena foreign and familiar.
www.whatarchitecture.com

CREDITS

All images and texts are courtesy the authors / artists unless otherwise stated.

Diagrams and photos on pages 9,18,25,27,173,175-177,179,185, 232-241,260-261,330 courtesy Anthony Hoete and WHAT Architecture.

"The Map is Not the Territory", all images are copyright the artists, courtesy England & Co Gallery, London. Simon Patterson, The Great Bear, courtesy Simon Patterson and Transport for London, photo: John Riddy.

"Automobilia", © Mother Advertising. First published as a promotional campaign for Q magazine.

"Truckworld", © Angus Carlyle. First published in Themepark issue 3: home, © 2001, Themepark.

"Scratched", Geoffrey de Crecey, reproduced courtesy of Solide Records Ltd. Paris.

"From a Cross to a Nought" © Eyal Weizman. First published in Yellow Rhythms, Diploma Project, Dip X 1988, Architectural Association School of Architecture.

"Zaha Hadid: Automobility and Architecture" was originally published in a reedited version as "The Taxi Interview" in Monument magazine. All images courtesy Zaha Hadid Architects, London. Interview courtesy of Zaha Hadid Architects. Photographs © Helene Binet. Portrait of Zaha Hadid © Jonathan De Villiers.

"Cinetrain", Laurie Hawkinson, originally published in: The Education of An Architect, Cooper Union, Rizzoli, 1988, Pages 228-232. © 1988 the Irwin S Chanin School of Architecture Cooper Union.

"Universal authority for National Flag Registration", UNFR, © 2000, Arjan Groot (020), first published by Anders NL, Amsterdam, The Netherlands

BLACK DOG
PUBLISHING UK

PHAIDON
PRESS US

100%

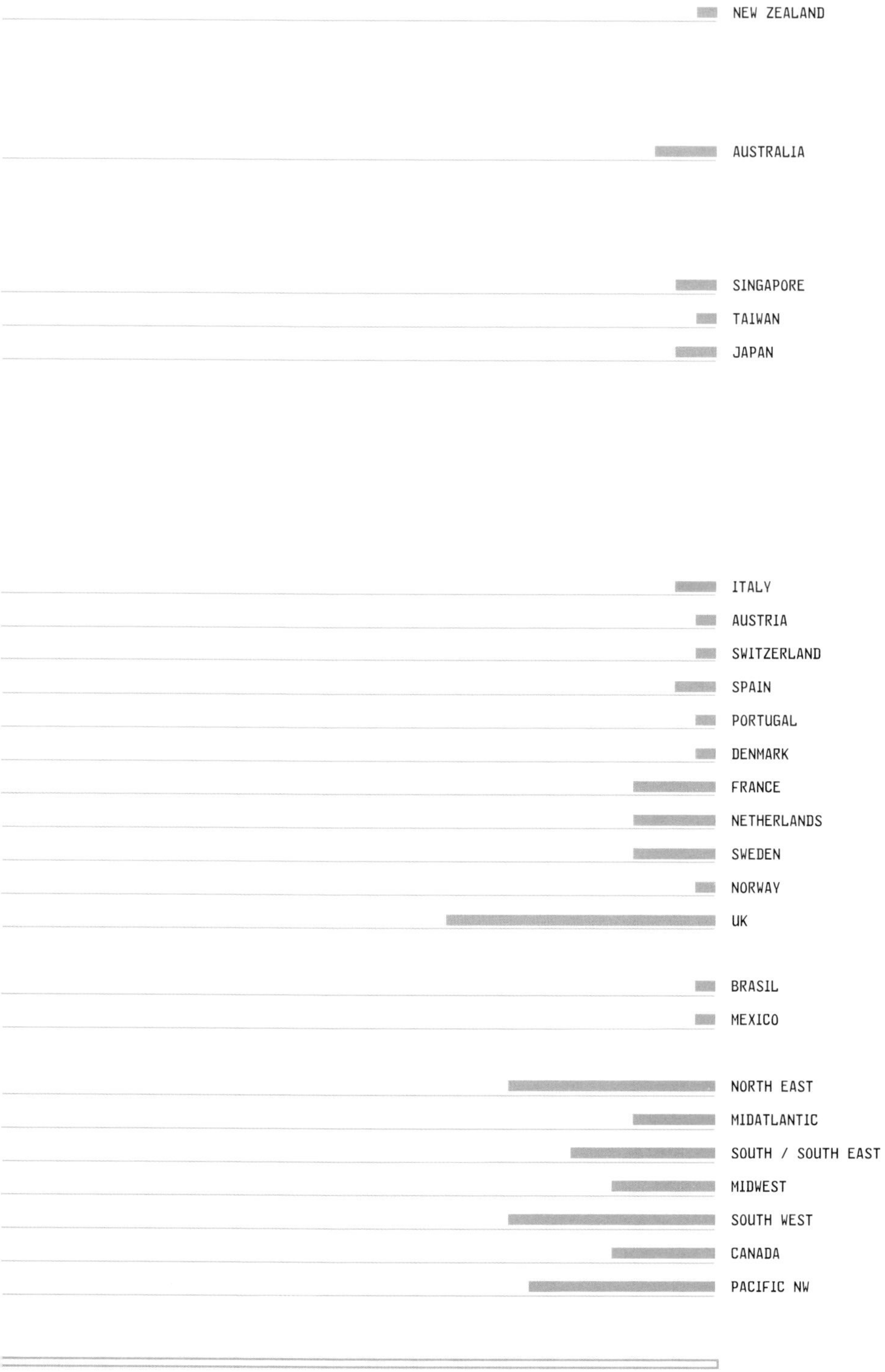

NEW ZEALAND

AUSTRALIA

SINGAPORE

TAIWAN

JAPAN

ITALY

AUSTRIA

SWITZERLAND

SPAIN

PORTUGAL

DENMARK

FRANCE

NETHERLANDS

SWEDEN

NORWAY

UK

BRASIL

MEXICO

NORTH EAST

MIDATLANTIC

SOUTH / SOUTH EAST

MIDWEST

SOUTH WEST

CANADA

PACIFIC NW

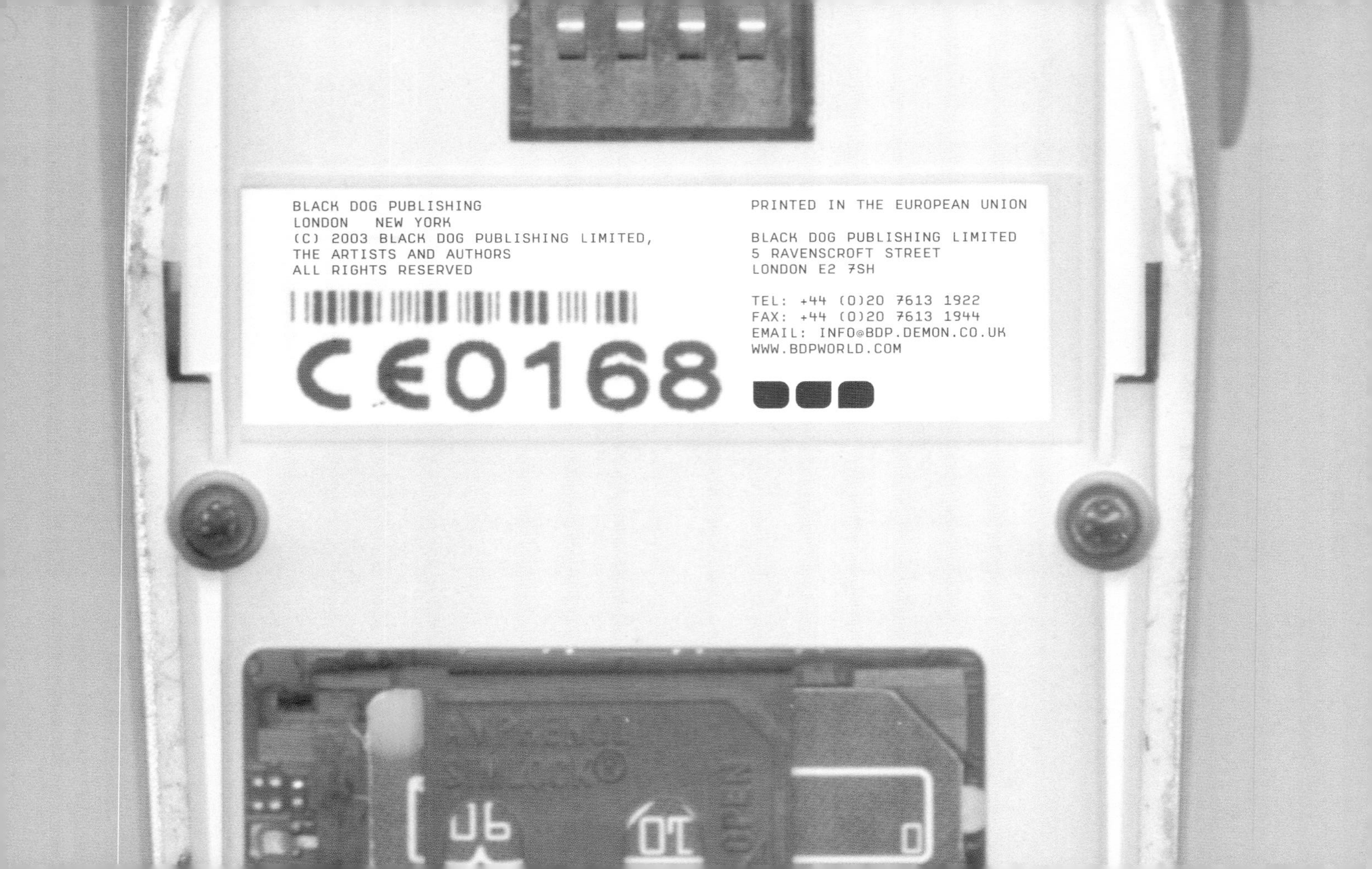
BLACK DOG PUBLISHING
LONDON NEW YORK
(C) 2003 BLACK DOG PUBLISHING LIMITED,
THE ARTISTS AND AUTHORS
ALL RIGHTS RESERVED
CE0168
PRINTED IN THE EUROPEAN UNION
BLACK DOG PUBLISHING LIMITED
5 RAVENSCROFT STREET
LONDON E2 7SH
TEL: +44 (0)20 7613 1922
FAX: +44 (0)20 7613 1944
EMAIL: INFO@BDP.DEMON.CO.UK
WWW.BDPWORLD.COM

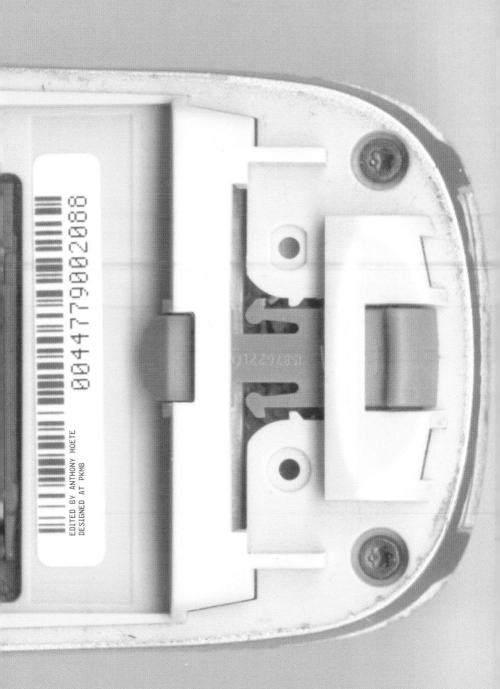

EDITED BY ANTHONY HOETE
DESIGNED AT PKMB

0044779002088

ISBN 1 901033 58 9
ROAM_V1
04.03